FAMILY AND CONSUMER SCIENCE 9
CHILD DEVELOPMENT AND CARE

CONTENTS

Author: **Marcia Parker, M.Ed.**
Editor: Alan Christopherson, M.S.
Illustrations: Alpha Omega Graphics

Alpha Omega Publications®

804 N. 2nd Ave. E., Rock Rapids, IA 51246-1759
© MM by Alpha Omega Publications, Inc. All rights reserved.
LIFEPAC is a registered trademark of Alpha Omega Publications, Inc.

CHILD DEVELOPMENT AND CARE

> *But Jesus called them unto him and said, Suffer little children to come unto me,*
> *and forbid them not: for of such is the kingdom of God.*
> ***Luke 18:16***

Children are certainly important to God as demonstrated in the above verse. We then have the responsibility to guide and train children in such a way that they will develop the correct view of God. This is one of the greatest challenges of parenthood: to teach children the truth about God. The home is the center of education, learning, and training for the child, so parents are given the responsibility of teacher. As an older sibling, babysitter, church nursery worker, Sunday School aide, or Vacation Bible School helper, you need to learn to meet the needs of children as well.

Children often give a first impression of being cute, spoiled, good, sad, naughty, shy, or quiet. Understanding the needs and behavioral development of children will help you to see past the first impression and will help you to develop a positive attitude toward all young children.

This LIFEPAC® is designed to increase your knowledge and understanding of children from birth to young school-age. You will study the physical, social, emotional, intellectual, and spiritual development of children by age groups. You will study and develop skills in child care and safety. You will also learn the business of babysitting.

OBJECTIVES

Read these objectives. The objectives tell you what you will be able to do when you have successfully completed this LIFEPAC.

When you have finished this LIFEPAC, you should be able to:

1. Identify the physical, social, emotional, intellectual, and spiritual development of children from birth to early school-age.

2. Develop the skills to care for each stage of a child's life from birth to young school-age.

3. Identify play as a child's way of exploring and learning about his world.

4. Identify music, art, literature, and science experiences as important to the development of young children.

5. Plan various activities for children.

6. Understand first aid and safety issues in child care.

7. Become a responsible and successful babysitter.

Note: All vocabulary words in this LIFEPAC appear in **boldface** print the first time they are used. If you are unsure of the meaning when you are reading, study the definitions given in the glossary.

I. AGES AND STAGES

And Jesus increased in wisdom and stature, and in favour with God and man.
Luke 2:52

Each child is unique. Each child will grow and learn at a different rate. Despite the individual differences, however, children of the same age develop in a similar manner. Understanding the physical, mental, social/emotional, and spiritual development of children gives you insight as to why a child behaves the way he does. When you realize that the child's behavior is partly determined by his age and stage in development, you can have more patience with the child; you can guide the child instead of becoming irritated with him.

This section will give you a brief overview of developmental and behavioral characteristics typical of each age group from birth to early school-age.

Section Objective

Review this objective. When you have completed this section, you should be able to:

1. Identify the physical, social, emotional, intellectual, and spiritual development of children from birth to early school-age.

PHYSICAL (STATURE)

Infants

Infants are unique individuals as much as any older person. Identical twins, born at the same time, will have different personalities. Some infants are very quiet and sleep often, while other infants are very active. Accepting these differences will make it easier to take care of infants and help them grow and develop. Adapt to each infant's behavior instead of expecting him to be like other infants.

Birth to six months. Infants increase rapidly in height, weight, and motor skills. At birth infants cannot control their body movements, as most of their movements are involuntary. During the first few months, an infant's eyesight is limited to objects that are about ten inches away from his face but by six months his range of vision is more fully developed. At about two months, infants can raise their bodies when lying on their stomachs. At three to four months, they discover their fingers, feet, and toes and have some control of their muscles and nervous system. They can sit with support, lift their heads up for short periods of time, and can roll from their sides to their stomachs. By five to six months, most babies can roll over.

Six to twelve months. Infants still nap in the morning and afternoon. They begin to eat and sleep at regular intervals. They will eat three meals a day and nurse or need a bottle at various times throughout the day. They start using a cup and a spoon to feed themselves. Infants can now sit unassisted. They crawl on their abdomens and creep on their hands and knees. By eight months, they can grasp and hold objects. They can pick up objects with their thumb and forefinger (the pincher grip) and let objects go (drop things); they even begin to throw things. At ten to twelve months they begin to pull themselves up to a vertical position, stand while holding furniture and can walk when led. By the time they are twelve months old, most babies weigh nearly three times their birth weight and are half-again longer.

Toddlers

When a child learns to walk, he is known as a toddler. Usually, this term is applied to one- and two-year-old children. The toddler stage is an important time in a child's life. It is the stage between infancy and childhood where they learn and grow in many ways. During the toddler stage, most children learn to walk, talk, solve problems, and relate to others. One major task for toddlers is learning to be independent.

One-year-olds. Toddlers may eat less but tend to eat more frequently throughout the day. They improve at feeding themselves, though spills should still be expected. They may grow less rapidly during this time than when they were infants. Most toddlers are walking without support by 14 months. Most can walk backwards, climb stairs, and run by 22 months. Toddlers can drink from cups with some help. They can scribble and stack blocks.

Two-year-olds. Two-year-olds are in constant motion, exploring their world with their bodies and senses. This helps develop their large motor skills. They are able to stand on tiptoes, throw a ball, and kick the ball forward. They can walk, run, climb, dig holes, and climb up and down stairs unassisted. They jump with two feet together. Two-year-olds will need large toys and plenty of room to explore. At this stage, they will begin to show an interest in toilet training and experience some success. They like to take things apart and put them back together. Because this may be their most active stage in life (thus the "terrible twos"), they still need an afternoon nap.

The preschooler. Three- and four-year-old children are often called preschoolers. Preschool children want to touch, taste, smell, hear, and test things for themselves. They are curious and eager to learn. They learn by experiencing, doing, and from their play. They are busy developing skills, using language and struggling to gain inner control.

Preschoolers want to assert their independence separate from their parents. They are more independent than toddlers. They have a better command of language and can better express their needs. Common fears of preschoolers include new places, experiences, and separation from parents and other important people.

The three-year-old. Three-year-olds are still developing their large motor skills. They are perfecting their running, jumping, hopping, climbing, and riding tricycles. They can catch balls, stand on one foot, and build towers of 6–9 blocks. They are beginning to learn hand-eye coordination with their small muscles (or fine motor skills). Provide them with toys and equipment that develop the fine motor skills, for example, puzzles, pencils, paper, and safety scissors. They can draw and paint in both circular and horizontal motions. Three-year-olds may still have toilet accidents. They like to dress themselves, but may or may not be able to manage buttons, snaps, and zippers. They grow about three inches taller in a year.

The four-year-old. Growth isn't as rapid for four-year-olds, yet they will grow taller losing some of their childish plumpness. Encourage them to participate in activities that will strengthen the large muscles in arms, legs, and trunks. They run on tip toes, gallop, and can pump themselves on a swing. They hop on one foot. They begin to skip. They throw a ball overhand. Their small muscles are developing, and hand-eye coordination is improving.

Four-year-olds can draw **representational** pictures (for example, pictures of flowers, people, etc.) They like unzipping, unsnapping, and unbuttoning clothes. They dress themselves. They are ready to learn how to tie their own shoes. They can cut on a line with scissors. They can make designs and write crudely-shaped letters. They are very active and aggressive in their play. Whether a child is right-handed or left-handed will be determined at about the age of four. Four-year-olds generally still need rest periods.

Young school-age

Five-, six-, and seven-year-old children are often excited about going to school and their new responsibilities. Parents are still the most important people in their lives. With school-age children, it is important to set limits and let children know what is expected of them. Do this with a soft voice. Be patient and kind. Provide clear and consistent discipline. Each child needs to feel special and cherished while in your care. Children in this stage are very enjoyable. They like to be helpful, especially to adults.

School-aged children become more agile.

Growth is slow but steady. They have good large muscle skills Most children have a good sense of balance and coordination. They can stand on one foot and walk on a balance beam. Some even have enough coordination to roller skate. They enjoy physical activities. They enjoy testing muscle strength and skills; they like to skip, run, tumble, and dance to music. Movements are often rough and jerky, but they love to learn new skills. They can catch small balls. They can better manage buttons and zippers and have learned to tie their shoelaces. They can print their names. They can copy designs and shapes, including numbers and letters. They use utensils and tools correctly without supervision. They have a good appetite and enjoy more adult foods. Afternoon naps are probably not necessary. Five-year-olds may need help with their toileting only if their clothes are complicated.

Answer *true* **or** *false.*

1.1 _____ Babies are unique individuals; different from other babies.

1.2 _____ Babies discover their fingers, feet, and toes at about five months.

1.3 _____ Children are called toddlers when they are toilet trained.

1.4 _____ Preschoolers are afraid to be separated from their parents.

1.5 _____ Young school-aged children should still take a nap.

Matching (answers may be used more than once).

1.6 _____ can sit unassisted

1.7 _____ can cut on a line with scissors

1.8 _____ most active stage in life

1.9 _____ likes to be helpful

1.10 _____ they grow about three inches taller in a year

1.11 _____ increases rapidly in height, weight, and motor skills

1.12 _____ right-handedness or left-handedness is determined

1.13 _____ learns to walk

1.14 _____ learning hand-eye coordination with their small muscles

a. birth to six months

b. six to twelve months

c. the one-year-old

d. the two-year-old

e. the three-year-old

f. the four-year-old

g. the young school-age

INTELLECT (WISDOM)

A child learns to speak what he hears. Encourage a child to pronounce words correctly; have him attempt to ask for things. Develop a love for good books and music by reading and singing to the child.

Birth to six months. At one month they become aware of normal household sounds. They turn to locate the source of sounds. Infants babble, coo, and gurgle; they smile. At three months they squeal, laugh, and babble. They study their hands and feet. Infants can focus on and follow moving objects with their eyes. They explore things with their mouths and put anything they can hold into their mouths. They cry in different ways to express hunger, anger, and pain. They forget about objects that they cannot see.

Six to twelve months. Infants wave bye-bye and play pat-a-cake. They respond to simple directions. They look for things not in sight. Infants make sounds like "dada" and "mama." They make sounds that are understood by people who know them well. They repeat actions that cause a response such as when given a rattle, they will shake it and laugh. By twelve months, many infants speak their first understandable words.

Read to the child.

The one-year-old. Toddlers add words to their vocabulary; they learn associations between words and objects; they name body parts and familiar pictures. They can point to objects that they want. They imitate animal sounds. They use the pronouns "me" and "mine." They use "no" frequently. They combine two words to make a basic sentence. They have short attention spans. They hold pencils and scribble.

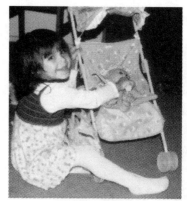

Twos enjoy imaginary play.

The two-year-old. Two-year-olds can understand more words than they can speak. They have a vocabulary of about three hundred words and can use three- to four-word sentences. They like to experiment with sounds and words. They still have short attention spans. Two-year-olds can follow simple directions and explanations. These will need to be repeated with patience. They can memorize short rhymes. They have begun imaginary play; for example, the two-year-old will "feed" their doll. They enjoy listening to short, simple stories. They want to make choices but find it difficult to do.

The three-year-old. Three-year-olds constantly ask questions. Almost one-third of their conversation is questions. They have a short attention span and enjoy having the same story read over and over. They enjoy riddles and guessing games. Three-year-olds have good imaginations and like pretending they are someone else: the doctor, the mommy, the daddy. They need toys that encourage imaginary play; for example, a cardboard box becomes a car, a boat, or a house. They may even have an imaginary playmate.

Threes have good imaginations.

The four-year-old. Attention spans of four-year-olds increase, so they can listen to longer stories. They ask many questions, including "how" and "why" questions. They are very talkative. Their language includes silly words and, if exposed to it, profanity. This would be a good time to explain why profanity is unacceptable. They enjoy serious discussions. They should understand some basic concepts such as number, size, weight, color, texture, distance, time, and position. Their classification skills and reasoning ability are developing. They are creative. They may still have an imaginary friend. They like rhythm and can follow a tune.

The young school-age. They can distinguish left from right. Their ability to speak and express themselves develops rapidly. This skill is important for success in school. They talk to their peers about themselves and their families. During play, they practice using the words and language they learn in school. They enjoy working with numbers, letters, words, and writing. They have a vocabulary of about two thousand words. They can begin to tell time and know the days of the week. They like silly rhymes, riddles, and jokes. Their attention span increases. They are learning more about their world and enjoy short field trips to the fire station, a construction site, or a zoo. They can follow more complicated stories. They are learning letters and words. By six, most can read words or combinations of words. Some misbehavior may be an indication of boredom.

They enjoy working with words.

Answer the following questions.

Remembering that each child develops at his own rate, identify intellectual characteristics that are common to the age groups. Write the *ages* next to the characteristic.

1.15 _____ likes to pretend

1.16 _____ likes to babble, coo, gurgle

1.17 _____ asks questions

1.18 _____ uses "no" frequently

1.19 _____ everything goes into the mouth

1.20 _____ has a short attention span

1.21 _____ begins to wave bye-bye

1.22 _____ has an imaginary playmate

 Answer *true* **or** *false*.

1.23 _____ Infants, one to six months, will turn towards the source of sound.

1.24 _____ Infants, six to twelve months of age will repeat actions that cause a response.

1.25 _____ Infants, six to twelve months, will name body parts.

1.26 _____ Two-year-olds have a vocabulary of about 500 words.

1.27 _____ Three-year-olds like to talk.

1.28 _____ Classification and reasoning skills begin at age four.

1.29 _____ Young school-age children have vocabulary of about 2,000 words.

1.30 _____ Some misbehavior in a school-age child may be an indication of boredom.

SOCIAL AND EMOTIONAL (FAVOR WITH MAN)

 **Birth to six months.** Infants begin to develop trust as their parents meet their needs: feeding them when they are hungry, holding and cuddling them when they cry, reading and singing to them, and changing their diapers when needed. They cry to express anger, pain, and hunger. Crying is their way of communicating. Infants are easily excited or frightened. They are easily upset and need to be cradled and comforted. Infants smile in response to a pleasant sound or a full tummy. At about six weeks, they smile in response to someone else. By four months, they smile broadly, laugh when pleased, and learn to recognize faces and voices of their parents.

Six to twelve months. At this time, infants start responding when you call their names. Separation anxiety begins at this point, they fear being left by their parents; they have a fear of strangers. They get angry and frustrated when their needs are not met in a reasonable amount of time. Infants begin to learn what is and is not allowed. Eye contact begins to replace some of the physical contact that younger infants seek.

The one-year-old. Temper tantrums are common, if allowed. They have difficulty sharing toys and are very possessive. They tend to have mood swings; their emotions are usually very intense but short-lived. Routines are very important. They enjoy playing in the presence of other children, but not with them. This is known as **parallel play**. In their view, they are the center of the world. They begin to express new emotions such as jealousy, affection, pride, and shame.

The two-year-old. Two-year-olds try to assert themselves by saying, "no." They like imitating the behavior of adults and other children. They enjoy solitary and parallel play much like the one-year-old. They are generally self-centered and sharing is still difficult. They become frustrated easily. They may be fearful of unfamiliar persons or animals, of being left alone, or of the dark. They may show this fear by crying, running away, clinging to the parent, or trembling. They still need security.

The three-year-old. Three-year-olds are usually interested in playing with other children or **cooperative play**. They are interested in sharing and taking turns. They have a definite choice of friends that they want to play with. They can be aggressive in words and actions. Three-year-olds may be afraid of the dark, of being alone, of getting lost, of unfamiliar places, buildings, animal sounds, or of being sick. They are struggling with the desire of being independent and the need for being close to family. It is a good time for them to experience being separated from family for short periods of time, as in a preschool or church program.

Threes take turns.

The four-year-old. Four-year-olds enjoy cooperative play. Generally, they do not get upset when separating from a parent in order to play with other children. They may have a best friend, but that changes frequently.

Fours enjoy cooperative play.

Most four-year-olds are friendly and enjoy talking to adults and desire adult approval. They also experience hero worship. Fours enjoy dramatic play and like to use props for dressing up and pretending. Expressing anger is common to four-year-olds. They develop fears about imaginary things such as giants, bears, or fires. They may fear pain or physical harm, for example, doctors, nurses, hospitals, or instruments. Four-year-olds have extreme mood swings; cheerful and cooperative one moment and sullen and uncooperative the next. Four-year-olds need support and guidance in understanding and expressing their "bad" feelings and in handling their own conflicts. Four-year-olds will develop an awareness of others' feelings; he may feel empathy for others.

The young school-age. Young school-age children like to play in small groups. They enjoy dramatic play and like to act grown up. They have a strong need to feel accepted and worthwhile. They show their ability to be independent by being disobedient, talking back, and being rebellious. They often express their anger by saying, "I hate you!" It is better not to yell back at the child. Remember Proverbs 15:1, "A soft answer turneth away wrath..." Acknowledge the child's anger, but do not allow him to get away with saying hurtful things. Boundaries must still be set. Instead say, "While I understand you are angry, you cannot say hurtful things to Mommy. Please sit on your bed for a few minutes until you are calm." Hug the child afterwards and assure him you still love him. In this way, the child is learning to control his outbursts.

Young school-age children prefer individual achievements over group efforts. They like encouragement and suggestions, but do not like to compete with other children. They still look to adults for approval but now they also turn to their peers for praise and acceptance. They begin to take responsibility for their own actions. They are beginning to learn to respect the rights and feelings of others. They look up to and imitate older youth. They are beginning to build and understand friendships; they now have a best friend.

Answer *true* **or** *false*.

1.31 _____ Infants are easily excited or frightened.

1.32 _____ By four months, an infant will realize when mom has entered the room.

1.33 _____ Infants, six to twelve months old, cannot yet determine what is and is not allowed.

1.34 _____ Routines are important to a one-year-old.

1.35 _____ The two-year-old understands the concept of sharing.

1.36 _____ The three-year-old is sometimes aggressive.

1.37 _____ The four-year-old often experiences hero worship.

1.38 _____ The young school-age child prefers solitary play.

Answer the following.

1.39 Distinguish between solitary, parallel, and cooperative play. _____

_____

_____

_____

_____

_____

1.40 What are some ways that parents can develop trust in their infants? _____

_____

_____

1.41 Emotional readiness to be separated from the family is developed in the _____

_____ .

1.42 Fear of imaginary things such as giants, bears, or fires develop in the _____

_____ .

1.43 "I hate you!" is a common expression of anger in the _____ .

9

SPIRITUAL (FAVOR WITH GOD)

Children of preschool-age learn quickly and generally do not question their teachers. They learn by observation, participation, and repetition. Sunday school is only a supplement to what is learned at home. Some of the helpful hints concerning methods for keeping the attention of small children during story time are: use visual aids (such as pictures), sit close to the children, speak with expression and enthusiasm.

Infants' concepts of God are gained through the love and care of the parent. Singing and listening to praise music with the infant will increase their appreciation for Christian music as they grow older. Your hugging, cradling, and loving care will open their heart to your instruction and Bible teachings in years to come.

Spiritual growth for the preschooler through the young school-age child is related to the child's growing awareness of self; such growth is almost entirely dependent on observation of the attitudes and behavior of those around him. Young children have an aptitude for Godly things. He is able to comprehend simple spiritual truths, such as:

An infant's concept of God is gained through the love of the parents.

1. God makes all good things, including the child.
2. God loves the child and is his best friend.
3. God listens when the child talks to Him (prayer).
4. God sees the child and is with him at all times.
5. God can do all things.

Two-year-olds. Two-year-olds can sense the attitudes of the home toward church. They sense something special about prayer or Bible reading or going to church. They can understand simple concepts about God; they enjoy singing simple songs about Jesus and friends.

Introduce Biblical concepts at the three-year-old stage.

The two-year-old may be interested in talking to God in his own manner. Observing others in prayer will help teach the child about prayer and God. It is not wise to force prayer, however. Instead, set an example by having regular prayer and devotional times.

Three-year-olds. It is easy for three-year-olds to talk about God. If they learn of God and Jesus at church or in the home, they will often bring God up in the conversation, for example, "God made the mountains."

Introduce the concept of God as a spirit and not just a man. Three-year-olds are beginning to use some simple Biblical principles, such as helpfulness and kindness. Read Bible stories of people who showed helpfulness or kindness to others (e.g. "The Good Samaritan") or teach a simple study in Galatians 5:22–23 on the fruit of the Spirit.

Four-year-olds. Four-year-olds are capable of talking to God in their own way. They are beginning to understand the concept of a personal God. They are learning to respond positively to people and things at church.

Young school-age. A young school-age child may be troubled because he cannot see God. They are inquisitive and may experience more abstract thoughts such as, "Where did God come from?"; "How long is eternity?" It is important to answer the children's questions as honestly as possible. This is how trust is developed.

Young school-age children are capable of using their own words to communicate with God. Therefore, it is important to encourage young children to pray on their own. They are growing in their understanding and application of Bible stories. They can memorize short Bible verses.

Encourage young children to pray on their own.

It is important to remember that each child is a separate individual, with ability, interest, and comprehension levels. One child may understand the concept of salvation at age four, while another may not comprehend it until much later. Some children may be able to memorize whole Bible verses and even passages at a very early age, while it may take other children longer to accomplish this task. Be patient and understanding in recognizing the differing abilities of children.

Answer the following questions.

1.44 How could you help teach the concept of kindness to a three-year-old child during Vacation Bible School? _____

_____

_____

_____

_____

1.45 Is it better to force a two-year-old to participate in grace at mealtimes or have him observe the family saying grace daily? Why? _____

_____

_____

_____

_____

_____

Complete the following activities.

Obtain permission from your church preschool director to observe children during Sunday School or during the week if your church has a day care or preschool program. You will need to visit a pre-school program three times while working in this LIFEPAC. When you observe children, you will need to do the following things.

Take your LIFEPAC and pencil with you to record your observations.

Remain in the background, give no indication of amusement, make no comment. Be an impartial observer.

Avoid conversation with the children or other observers.

Place your chair so you are not in the way of the children and do not block any of the play things.

Avoid disturbing the children's activities by coming and going.

1.46 **Observation number one: Observing a group of children.** As you observe the children in the group, see how many patterns of behavior you can identify.

Date _____ Place _____ Length of time _____
Age(s) of Children _____

a. Notice the following:

1. Children who seem to trust adults _____

_____

_____

2. Children who have many interests and engaged in a variety of activities _____

_____

_____

3. Children who seem to limit their activities and interests _____

_____

_____

4. Children who combine materials in unusual ways _____

_____

_____

5. Children who engage freely in dramatic play _____

_____

_____

6. Children who seem dependent on others, who follow the teacher or other students around, or frequently ask for help _____

_____

_____

7. Children who seem to like many children and approach them freely _____

_____

_____

8. Children who seem to avoid approaching children _____

_____

_____

b. Make a list of the things children do which you dislike. _____

_____

_____

c. Make a list of the things children do that make you want to step in and do something about their behavior. _____

_____

_____

d. Make a list of the things children do that you approve of or which you enjoy seeing them do.

_____

_____

e. Discuss your observations with your teacher and classmates when back in class.

 Adult Check _____

                                                   Initial   **Date**

1.47 **Observation number two: Observe one child.** Choose one child and observe his behavior without his knowing he is being watched. Make sure you get permission before doing your observation.

Date _____ Place _____ Length of time _____
Name of child _____ Age of Child _____

a. How many different activities did he engage in during the period and for how long?

Activity   **Length of Time**

_____

_____

_____

_____

_____

_____

_____

_____

b. Did he play contentedly and satisfactorily with others?

_____

c. Did he play contentedly by himself?

_____

d. With whom did he play?

_____

e. What toys did he use?

_____

f. When he changed from one activity to another, what were the reasons for the change?

_____

g. Did he get out his toys?

_____

h. Did he put them away when finished with them?

_____

i. Was he bossy?

_____

j. Did he interfere with the play of other children? If he interfered, what action did he take?

_____

k. Was he selfish? In what way was he selfish?

_____

_____

l. Was he generous? How was this demonstrated?

_____

m. Was he shy?

_____

n. Did he show off? If he did show off, what did he do?

_____

o. Was he happy?

_____

p. Was he quarrelsome?

_____

q. Was he sympathetic? If he was, how did he show it?

_____

r. Did he tease and annoy others? If so, in what way?

_____

s. Was he cooperative? If so, how was this demonstrated?

_____

t. Was there any kind of discipline used? Give an example. Was it desirable? What other means
   of discipline might have been better used? _____

_____

_____

u. What conclusions do you draw concerning the characteristics of the child you observed?

_____

_____

_____

v. Discuss your observations with your teacher and classmates when back in class.

Adult Check _____

                            Initial   **Date**

Review the material in this section in preparation for the Self Test. The Self Test will check
your mastery of this particular section. The items missed on this Self Test will indicate specific
areas where restudy is needed for mastery.

SELF TEST 1

Answer *true* **or** *false* (each answer, 3 points).

1.01 _____ The four-year-old still needs a rest period.

1.02 _____ Young school-age children begin taking responsibility for their actions.

1.03 _____ Answering questions correctly helps develop a sense of trust in a child.

1.04 _____ The two-year-old is old enough to share his toys.

1.05 _____ Babies discover their fingers, feet, and toes at about twelve months.

1.06 _____ Children are called toddlers when they begin to walk.

1.07 _____ Infants, six to twelve months of age, will repeat actions that cause a response.

1.08 _____ Four-year-olds have a vocabulary of about 2,000 words.

1.09 _____ In a young school-age child, misbehavior maybe an indication of boredom.

1.010 _____ Three-year-olds are not ready to be separated from their family.

Match the behavior to the appropriate age group. Some answers will be used more than once (each answer, 4 points).

1.011 _____ solitary play

1.012 _____ has a best friend

1.013 _____ begins to feel empathy

1.014 _____ three-hundred word vocabulary

1.015 _____ constantly asks questions

1.016 _____ curious and eager to learn

1.017 _____ enjoys short field trips

a. two-year-old

b. three-year-old

c. four-year-old

d. young school-age

Fill in the blank (each answer, 5 points).

1.018 Understanding the physical, _____ , social, _____ , and _____ development of children will give you insights into why a child behaves the way he does.

1.019 The baby increases rapidly in height, _____ and _____ .

1.020 Two spiritual truths that the preschooler is able to comprehend are _____ and _____ .

16

Essay (answer, 7 points).

1.021   How does the Principle of Individuality apply to our study of the ages and stages of children?

_____

_____

_____

_____

_____

80 / 100

Score _____

Adult Check _____

Initial   Date

II. CARE OF CHILDREN

> *...but bring them up in the nurture and admonition of the Lord.*
> ***Ephesians 6:4b***

The basic needs of children of all ages are food, sleep, warmth, and loving attention. Learning techniques and developing skills in child care and safety will be a major portion of this section of the LIFEPAC.

Learning to entertain children with quality, positive activities is also important in their proper development. You will study and participate in creative learning activities for the preschool child and young school-age child.

Section Objectives

Review these objectives. When you have completed this section, you should be able to:

2.   Develop the skills to care for each stage of a child's life from birth to young school-age.

3.   Identify play as a child's way of exploring and learning about his world.

4.   Identify music, art, literature, and science experiences as important to the development of young children.

5.   Plan various activities for children.

BASIC INFANT CARE

When picking your baby up, whether to change his diaper, bathe him or feed him, always hold him firmly and confidently and talk to him softly and gently, making eye contact.

Picking up your baby. Holding and cuddling your baby makes him feel safe and loved. When lifting up your baby, remember the head and back need proper support.

Step One: As you stand facing the baby, slide one hand up and under a shoulder to support the neck and head. The other hand should be up and under the hips on the opposite side of the baby to support the back.

Step Two: Lift him gently and slowly toward your chest. Turn him so that his head is cradled in the crook of your elbow and his body is supported along the length of your arm.

Step Three: When you put him down, support his head and bottom. Slide your hand out from under his bottom first, then from beneath his head.

Holding your baby. There are several ways that babies like to be held, but a newborn cannot support his head, so always support his neck to stop his head from flopping back.

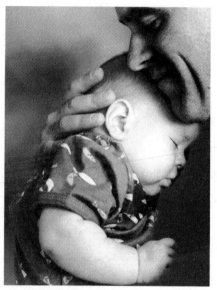

Cuddle him close against your shoulder with one hand supporting the head and neck and the other under his bottom. Hold him upright to look over your shoulder.

Cradle him lengthwise in your arms, keeping his head supported.

Bathing your baby. When bathing a baby, never leave the baby alone for even a few seconds; a baby can drown in less than an inch of water. Collect everything you need before you start, including a baby bathtub or sink, washcloth, towel, soap/shampoo, cotton swabs and balls, brush and comb, diaper, and a complete change of clothing. The room temperature should be about 75 degrees Fahrenheit.

Put cold water in the bathtub first, followed by hot, and test the temperature with your elbow. The water should be warm but not too hot. Undress the baby and gently lower him into the tub, supporting his head and back. Keep one arm under his shoulders at all times. With your free hand, wash his face first, then wash and rinse his hair and body. Slide your free arm under his bottom and lift him out gently. Wrap him in a towel and pat him dry. Keep the baby covered while you dress him and put on a clean diaper.

Dressing your baby. Choose soft, comfortable clothes with no irritating tags or seams. They should be made simply without collars, ribbons, ruffles, or lace. Select clothing that comes off and on easily. Make sure outfits open easily at the crotch for diaper changes. Most babies dislike having clothes pulled over their heads. If you have to put a shirt on over the head of the baby, follow these three steps.

- Gather the shirt at the neck with the front facing you. Place the back of the shirt at the top of the baby's head.

- Gently raise his head and slip the shirt over his face, taking care not to drag it. Pull the shirt down over his neck and shoulders and lower him down.

- Gather up the sleeve with one hand, stretch the opening wide and holding the baby's wrist, guide his arm through. Repeat with the other arm. Pull it down behind his back.

To help prevent diaper rash, change the baby's diaper as soon as it becomes wet or soiled. You may find that newborn babies need changing 10–12 times a day. When changing a baby's diaper, never leave the baby alone for even a few seconds. Changing a baby's diaper should be done as follows:

- Lie the baby down on a changing mat or other flat surface. Remove the old diaper. Lift his legs up by the ankles with one hand and use a moist wipe to clean off the worst of any soiling. Roll up the old diaper, folding the soiled part inward and put it and the wipe in a plastic bag.

- Thoroughly clean the whole area, wiping from front to back with a clean, dampened washcloth or moist cotton balls. Wipes are harsh for a newborn but fine for older infants.

- When his bottom is clean and dry, apply a **barrier cream** to his bottom. Lift his legs up by the ankles with one hand and slide an open diaper under him with the other hand. Boys need the most bulk in the front and girls need the most bulk in the back.

- Secure the clean diaper. If you are using a disposable diaper, secure with the taped tabs. If you are using a cloth diaper and pins, put your fingers between the baby and the diaper to avoid sticking him with the pin. Pin from the front to the back on both sides to prevent possible injury to internal organs.

Feeding your baby. There are two choices for feeding a newborn baby: breast feeding and bottle feeding. The choice is a personal one. Breast feeding offers many benefits for both mother and baby that formula milk is unable to duplicate. But for those who decide not to breast feed, formula milk provides all the nutrients a baby needs.

If the baby is breast fed, never substitute milk or formula without the parent's directions. Begin **weaning** the baby from the bottle around six months of age. While the baby is still being breast fed, the use of a bottle for supplementary liquids such as diluted apple or white grape juice is a good beginning step. Introduce a cup to the infant at this age.

If the baby is bottle fed, there is a wide choice of commercially-made formula milk to choose from. To avoid infection, all equipment must be thoroughly cleaned and sterilized. Some babies drink formula warm and some right out of the refrigerator, depending on age and preference. If heating the formula, always check the temperature of the formula before giving it to the baby. Let a few drops fall on the inside of your wrist. If it's comfortably warm it should be okay for the baby.

BENEFITS OF BREAST MILK[1]

Breast milk contains the correct proportion of nutrients needed for growth and development in the first few months of life. It is the right temperature, does not need sterilizing equipment and is free and readily available.

Antibodies help to protect the baby against infections such as vomiting and diarrhea, coughs and colds, and urinary and ear infections.

Breast milk may reduce the risk of Sudden Infant Death Syndrome (SIDS), helps prevent juvenile diabetes, and protects against allergies. Some studies have found that breast-fed children have better dental health, fewer bowel problems, and fewer speech problems than formula-fed babies.

Breast-feeding helps you develop a close bond with your baby, regain your figure more quickly, and may reduce the risk of developing breast and ovarian cancer in later life.

1 This table was adapted from <u>You and Your Baby</u>, by Gila Leiter, M.D. and Allen Babbitz, M.D.

Find a comfortable chair and hold the baby with his head supported in your arm. The head needs to be higher than the rest of his body. Relax and talk to him while he is eating. Tip the bottle to make sure the nipple is always filled with liquid. This prevents air from getting into the baby's stomach.

Make sure to burp the baby during and after the feeding. This helps get out the air that has built up in his stomach. Put a cloth diaper or towel over your shoulder. Lift the baby against your shoulder or sit the infant on your lap. Gently but firmly pat the infant's back to get up the air bubbles. The infant may spit up some formula. Don't worry, this is normal.

Bibs, bottles, messy faces, spitting up, and food on the floor are all part of feeding a baby. Yet, it can also be a fun time. Put the baby in a safe place while you are gathering everything you need. When feeding the baby, relax. A baby can sense if you are nervous.

Rice cereal is usually the first solid food that a baby eats. When the baby is ready for food that takes more chewing, he might eat cooked fruits and vegetables (mashed with a fork), dry cereals and bread or crackers in bite sized pieces.

Hold baby in a sitting position or put him in a high chair. Use a small, thin spoon to fit the baby's mouth. Put a little food on the spoon. Put the food toward the back of the baby's mouth. The baby may spit out the food. This is because he may not know how to chew it. Give the baby another bite even if he spits out the first bite. If the baby will not eat something, do not force him. Wait and try feeding him later.

After the baby has acquired his four front teeth (the central incisors) which erupt between six and eight months, a mother can gradually introduce foods with lumpy consistencies.

Toddlers are ready for bite sized food.

Finger foods at meal and snack time help in the development of hand-to-mouth (or hand-eye) coordination, a necessary skill for him to become a self-feeder, later.

Babies need sleep. Every child's sleep needs are different. A newborn may sleep as much as 20 hours out of every 24. By the time he is six months old, he will sleep about sixteen hours a day; eleven or twelve at night, along with a morning and afternoon nap. By the time he is one, the morning naps are usually shortened until dropped. Naps usually cease during the later preschool and young school-age years, ages three to six, but quiet time is still recommended.

Younger infants generally sleep when they are tired. Some infants have difficulty relaxing and settling down to sleep. Some infants get over-tired and then have trouble sleeping. Older infants usually have a routine—something that the parent does each time the child is put to sleep. It is not always easy to put an infant to sleep. Do not be surprised if it takes a great deal of time. You can play soft, calm music or gently pat the child on the back and hum to settle or relax the child. If the child cries a little bit, but remains laying on the bed, try being quiet in the room or leave quietly. Do not let the child cry for more than just a few minutes before you go in and help. If the child stands up or cries a lot, help the child relax and settle down to sleep.

Answer the following questions.

2.1 When picking up or holding a baby, you need to support the _____ and
_____ .

2.2 What is the first step to bathing a baby? _____
_____

2.3 How do you test the temperature of the bath water? _____

2.4 What is the first area of the baby's body that you wash? _____

2.5 Describe the best type of clothing for a baby. _____
_____
_____

2.6 How often should you change a baby's diaper? _____

2.7 When removing a soiled diaper or replacing a clean diaper, how do you lift the baby's bottom up?
_____

2.8 What is a barrier cream? _____

2.9 List the two choices for feeding a newborn baby. _____ and
_____ . Which is recommended as being the best method and
why? _____
_____
_____

2.10 Define weaning. _____
_____

2.11 Why is it important to burp a baby during and after the feeding? _____
_____

2.12 What is the first solid food that a baby will most likely eat? _____

2.13 Why are finger foods important to the development of the child? _____
_____

2.14 How many hours a day might a six month old infant sleep? _____

Complete the following activity.

2.15 Change a baby's diaper. You should be able to change a cloth diaper as well as a disposable diaper.
If you do not have a live baby to work on, then use a life sized doll.

Adult Check _____
Initial   Date

HUGS—THE WONDER DRUG

Have you ever wondered how effective hugs are? You rarely give a hug that is not appreciated, or receive one that does not make your day a little brighter. Can you think of any medication that has such pleasant side effects?

Hugs are good for you. They're not fattening and they contain no preservatives, artificial sweeteners, or other chemical additives. Hugs are cholesterol free and contain 100% of the recommended daily allowance of hope and happiness. They are a completely renewable source of energy and are available without a prescription!

They are particularly effective in treating everyday problems such as stress, worry, anger, frustration, sadness or sorrow, and even an occasional nightmare.

The best thing about hugs is that you can use them without special training or prior experience. But a word of caution for those trying it for the first time: **You should never wait until tomorrow to hug someone who needs it today!** Once you realize how good it feels, you'll want to do it all over again.

CAUTION: HUGS ARE EXTREMELY ADDICTIVE!

–Source Unknown

CREATIVE CHILD CARE

Toddlers, preschoolers, and young school-age children also need plenty of love and attention. They are beginning to learn who they are and what their capabilities are. Every day is an adventure to the toddler, preschooler, and young school-age child. They are becoming more independent, but still desire (and need) the help and guidance of the parents.

Children need to be held.

Holding your child. Toddlers, preschoolers, and young school-age children still need to be held. They enjoy sitting close to an adult for story time or family time. They appreciate the value of a good hug, too.

Bathing your child. When bathing older children, make sure that they sit still in the tub. Children can slip and fall if they are standing or moving around. You will need to help young children in cleaning themselves and in washing their hair. Be careful not to get shampoo in their eyes while rinsing their hair. Never leave a child alone in the bathtub for any reason! Children have been known to drown in only a couple inches of water.

Make bath time fun.

Fill the tub to the proper temperature before you allow the child to get in. Allow the child to play in the tub for awhile to make the bathing experience fun. Provide bath toys and bubble bath. Young children really enjoy bubbles; you can make facial beards, blow them, and have great fun with them. While the shampoo is still in the hair, forming shapes and funny hairdos is an entertaining activity that will make washing hair a more positive experience for the child.

Begin toilet training children close to their second birthday. The parent must see that the child understands what is expected of them and then carry out a routine. Be consistent. Never leave a child on the potty chair alone and never for more than five minutes at a time. Commend success, but don't reprimand failure. Most children are day trained by age 2 1/2, but may not be fully trained at night.

Once the child reaches the age of about four or five, he can participate in his own grooming. He can brush his teeth, be taught to clean his hands and fingernails, and can attempt to comb his own hair. He can learn to blow his own nose and be discouraged from picking his nose.

Dressing your child. Most toddlers will need help dressing. Some toddlers would prefer to do it themselves. Most toddlers and preschoolers still need some assistance in zipping zippers and buttoning buttons. A few preschoolers will learn to tie their shoes before they reach kindergarten age.

Be practical in selecting your child's wardrobe. Buy soft, comfortable, easy-to-wash clothes made out of durable, long-lasting materials for everyday wear and playtime. Save the fancy dresses and suits for church.

Preschool children enjoy making choices. You can help them choose sock colors, certain outfits, or what to wear in their hair or on their head. It is okay, however, for them to go out to play wearing outfits that do not match. Allow them to express their individuality. The same goes with the young school-age children.

Feeding your child. Toddlers enjoy finger foods because they are easier to grasp. Give a toddler child size utensils as they are easier for the toddler to manipulate. All children are messy eaters and they often spill. Learning table manners and how to use forks and spoons correctly takes time. Use child-sized plastic cups, plates, and bowls to prevent broken dishes.

Toddlers can eat three meals a day plus healthy snacks in between so that they eat every two or three hours. Make sure that all food is cut into bite-size pieces for easy chewing. You will also want to make sure that a toddler sits still while eating to prevent choking hazards.

Children differ in their needs for food and their surrounding food. Some are hearty eaters, while others are very picky. Some children always eat big meals, others eat small amounts often throughout the day. Given the chance, most children do a good job of eating the food they need.

Serve child-sized portions so that the child can finish before getting too full. A good rule is one level tablespoon of food for each year of age. For example, a three-year-old would get three tablespoons each of several different healthy foods. If in doubt, always start small, you can always give a second helping if he eats the first.

Do not force a child to eat if he does not seem hungry. A child who is going through a time of slow growth or who has been inactive or ill may not be hungry. Be aware that even with your best efforts, there may be times when the child just doesn't eat. This is not unusual for preschoolers and school-age children. If it only happens from time to time, then you need not worry.

Set a good example. Children are great imitators and they watch what you do, so eat healthy foods as well.

Small children are dependent on the people in charge of them to provide them with a healthy diet. It is easy to eat foods that will give the child lots of energy and help them stay healthy. The best way to eat right is to follow the USDA MyPlate guidelines.

Recommended amounts for young children are as follows:

Fats, Sweets, and Oils. These items are not considered to be a food group. Oils are liquid at room temperature. Oils are necessary in limited amounts for good health. Fats are solid at room temperature. Candy, cookies, fudge...all children love these foods, but they are not very good for them. Sweets are empty calories—they are high in fat and calorie content and return little nutritional value. They should only be eaten once in a while and in small amounts.

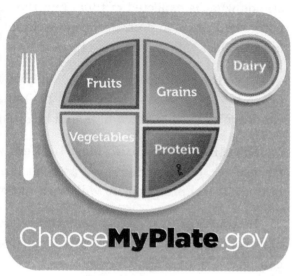

The 2011 MyPlate

Dairy Group. While some Dairy Group items have a lot of fat, they also have protein and calcium. Children should have 2 cups from the Dairy Group every day in portions such as low fat milk (1 cup), low fat yogurt (1 cup), or natural cheese (1 1/2 ounces). Toddlers up to age two may drink whole milk. Their growing bodies need the extra fat.

Milk is called "the almost perfect food" and is very important for the growing child. Milk contains complete proteins for building muscles and body tissues; calcium, phosphorus, and Vitamin D for building strong bones and teeth; and easily digested fat and sugar for energy.

Avoid forcing the child to drink milk. When a child balks at drinking milk, try serving it in another form. Milk can be served as a beverage; used in cereals, soups, puddings, tapioca, custard, and ice cream or cheese. Milk can also be flavored to make it more appetizing. Also, many children enjoy eating fruit-flavored yogurt.

Some children are allergic to cow's milk. If you are caring for someone else's child, always check with the parents when in doubt about serving milk. Children who are allergic to cow's milk must get milk's nutrition from other sources, such as soy milk.

Protein Group. This group includes beef, poultry, fish, dry beans, eggs, and nuts. It could be called the protein group. It's important to eat 5 oz. of these foods every day so that they will have the energy to grow and play.

Fruits Group. Fruits are sweet and delicious. Apples, oranges, grapes, and bananas make great snacks any time of day. These and other fruits also contain many important vitamins to ward off colds and other illnesses. One and a half cups of fruit is recommended every day.

Vegetables Group. Vegetables have important vitamins and minerals to make children stronger. Carrots, lettuce, peppers, peas...vegetables keep children healthy! It is important to eat a wide variety in this group, as they do not contain the same nutrients or **phytochemicals**. The young child needs to eat plenty of these great foods, around two and a half cups every day.

Grains Group. Grains are the cornerstone of any healthy diet. Carbohydrates such as bread, cereal, crackers, rice, and pasta, are readily absorbed by the body, so foods containing them provide great short-term energy. It is important to eat a lot of these foods, 6 oz. every day.

Snacking is an important part of the young child's diet. Be sure to choose nutritious snacks instead of ones with empty calories. Snacks provide needed energy and nutrition for the young child.

A child needs sleep. Older children need a bedtime routine. They need to go to bed at the same time every night. They need to go to bed early because they will be early to rise. A nightly "ritual" is usually good to establish so they know what is expected of them.

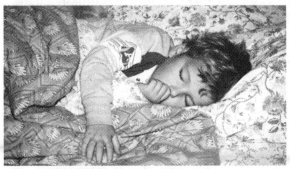

Toddlers prefer playing to sleeping. Help the child calm down first by reading books or laying down next to them and telling a comforting story. Generally, toddlers do not need to cry before they sleep, so be sure you calm the child down sufficiently before putting him to sleep.

For the preschool child, keep activities calm before nap time or bed time. For safety reasons, make sure you are available while the child is settling down to sleep. Preschool children can get up and may get into unsafe situations. Relax, read books, and play imaginary games to help the preschooler close his or her eyes. Imagine sitting by a river or watching clouds in the sky.

Reading to a child before bedtime helps her relax.

School-age children often like to read before they go to sleep. Sometimes they like to be read to and sometimes they like to read by themselves. This helps them relax. If the child has had a very active day, it might be difficult to calm down enough to sleep. You might need to do calming activities like listening to calm music or playing lying-down games using their imagination. For instance, imagine soaring above the clouds—what would it feel like? Some children might be too excited because you are there. You might assure them that when they wake up, their parents will be home.

The ideal sleeping arrangements would include the following. A child should sleep in a separate room from the parents after infancy. Children of opposite sex should be in separate rooms by the time the oldest child enters school. Each child should sleep alone in a bed, even in a shared room.

Your child needs spiritual guidance. At the beginning of this section of the LIFEPAC, you were given a verse from the Bible with instructions on how to meet your child's spiritual needs.

> *...but bring them up in the nurture and admonition of the Lord.* ***Ephesians 6:4b***

The word *nurture* involves counseling and training, and the word *admonition* involves reproof, correction, and encouragement.

Parents need to build a foundation of strong character into the lives of their children. Instant and cheerful obedience is an inward positive attitude and an outward compliance with the requests made by God, parents, and others in authority.

> *Children obey your parents in the Lord: for this is right.* ***Ephesians 6:1***

> *Children obey your parents in all things: for this is wellpleasing unto the Lord.*
> ### *Colossians 3:20*

Submission is an act of yielding to the authority of another. A child's will needs to be brought lovingly and consistently into submission to the parent. This must be learned in the toddler stage: 18 months. Failure to learn this principle in the home creates problems at school, at work, and in future homes. Jesus Christ submitted to His Father's will when He died for us (Luke 22:42).

Your child needs discipline. Discipline is defined as the efforts of parents to train, control, and remedy the actions of their children to help them toward their best all-around development. Discipline can be divided into three areas. First, children need thorough and explicit instruction on what is expected of them. Boundaries must be set; rules must be established. The child needs to know what discipline will be administered for what broken rule. For example, the child should be spanked for direct disobedience or rebellion. Second, parents should control and reinforce this instruction. They must see that the child stays within the boundaries set and adheres to the rules established. Third, parents should administer any necessary correction needed to bring the child back within the boundary lines.

REASONS FOR MISBEHAVIOR[2]

All children misbehave sometimes. That is a normal part of growing up. But, children's behavior is sometimes influenced strongly by the people and environment around them. Here are some reasons a child may be misbehaving:

- ✓ Needs a nap
- ✓ Feels ill
- ✓ Needs to eat or drink
- ✓ Is overstimulated
- ✓ Feels bored
- ✓ Feels frustrated
- ✓ Feels scared around strangers
- ✓ Needs to feel a sense of power and control
- ✓ Needs attention

For the younger child, the disciplinary action should be taken immediately after the infraction because they have short memories. For example, if a child disobeys in a public place, quickly find a private place and deal with the problem. If you wait until you get back home, the child will not understand why he is being scolded because he has forgotten what he did. For preschool and school-age children, you can write down on a piece of paper at the store what the child did. Show him the paper and say, "I am writing down that you disobeyed me by touching this glass vase after I told you not to. When we get home I will read this note to you and will punish you. Do you understand?"

Any act of discipline should be done in private; a bedroom, bathroom, etc. It needs to be done in love and gentleness. Never discipline a child while you are angry.

Ask the child the following questions:

- ➢ What did you do and why did you do it?
- ➢ What should you have done?
- ➢ What did I say I would do if that happened?
- ➢ What am I going to have to do?

Once the child clearly understands what he has done and the consequences for his actions, administer the disciplinary action and make sure the child knows he has been forgiven and is loved. The child needs to ask forgiveness from God.

---

2 Adapted from the Urban Programs Resource Network, The University of Illinois Extension Program, *A guide to the business of babysitting.*

PREVENTING MISBEHAVIOR[3]

You can prevent some misbehavior of children from occurring by practicing some of the following tips:

✔ Use encouraging words—When children are behaving well, they deserve your attention and appreciation. They will learn that good behavior is a way to be noticed.

✔ Use positives—Tell children what you want them to do rather than what you do not want them to do. Changing "Don'ts" to "Do's" takes practice, but is worth the effort. "Do's" give positive ideas rather than negative ones and are more easily understood.

✔ Set limits—Limits tell a child what is expected. Too many rules and demands may overwhelm a young child, but setting a few limits on matters that are really important reduces conflict and the need for making more discipline decisions. Limits are most effective when they match a child's ability; are expressed in clear, positive terms; are consistently enforced; and are based on reasons the child understands. Example: The child can no longer sleep at naptime but becomes overtired by the end of the day. Insist that he spend an hour doing quiet activities after lunch.

✔ Give choices—When children are allowed to make small choices (Examples: An apple or raisins for snack, television or a story before bed) they learn to make simple decisions and will be prepared to make more important decisions in the future. They feel a sense of power and control over their lives when they can make some choices.

✔ Use humor—Children respond well to humor. It is effective at breaking tension or avoiding a struggle. (Example: The child has left his jacket outside. You say, "I see a lost jacket out in the yard. I hope someone helps that poor jacket find its way home.")

✔ Warnings—Letting a child know in advance what to expect eases transitions and reduces resistance. (Example: The children are busy playing. You let them know that lunch will be ready in ten minutes.)

✔ Plan ahead—Be prepared so that problem behavior is avoided. (Example: You know the child becomes irritable when he gets bored so you pack some toys and activities to play with when this child is in your care.)

✔ Change the setting—Change the child's environment so that certain misbehaviors are prevented. (Example: The toddler likes to tear up newspapers so you put the newspaper out of sight.)

✔ Role model—Practice the behavior you would like the children in your care to adopt. (Example: You want the child to let someone finish speaking so you do not interrupt the child when he speaks.)

3 Adapted from the Urban Programs Resource Network, The University of Illinois Extension Program, *A guide to the business of babysitting.*

Answer the following questions.

2.16 How can you make taking a bath and washing hair fun for the young child? _____

_____

_____

2.17 By the age of four, a child can help participate in the following grooming activities: _____

_____

_____ .

2.18 The best way to eat properly is to follow the _____ .

2.19 A young child should have _____ of oils, fats, or sweets, _____ cups from the
dairy group, _____ oz. from the protein group, _____ cups from the vegetables group,
_____ cups from the fruits group, and _____ oz. from the grains group every day.

2.20 The three areas of discipline are: _____

_____

_____

2.21 Why is it important to discipline the young child as soon after the infraction as possible?

_____

_____

2.22 Any discipline should be done in _____ , in love, and _____ .

Answer *true* **or** *false*.

2.23 _____ Young school-age children still need hugs.

2.24 _____ Most children are toilet trained by age two.

2.25 _____ A young child just learning to dress himself should be expected to wear matching
clothes.

2.26 _____ Children have different eating habits and needs.

2.27 _____ Force a child to drink milk, so he receives the number of servings needed for good
health.

2.28 _____ To tire him out, play a rowdy game of wrestling with your child before putting him
to bed.

2.29 _____ A child needs to learn submission during the preschool stage of his growth.

ACTIVITIES

Play is the main business of childhood. It is the way children develop alert, imaginative minds and build strong bodies. They learn to get along with others. Children learn about their world and develop coordination and **manipulative skills** through play. Children participate in **creative play**, **imaginative play**, **adventure play**, manipulative play, and **secondhand learning**. Each kind of play is important at different stages of children's development.

Toys. Toys are an important part of play. Each child can benefit from an assortment of toys designed for his age level.

Two-year-olds. Provide playthings that can be taken apart and put together easily, such as a nest of blocks. Large pegboards and push-pull toys are suitable. Two-year-olds also like stuffed animals and dolls, bath toys, blocks, sandbox with digging toys, small table and chairs, and wheel toys.

Three-year-olds. The three-year-old needs toys he can experiment with and share with his friends. Appropriate toys include building blocks, wooden animals, kiddy cars or tricycles, finger paints, clay, play dough, cars and wagons, wheelbarrows, rocking horses, picture books, and crayons.

Four-year-olds. Toys which encourage make-believe aid in learning. Select small brooms, carpet sweepers, garden tools, doctor or nurse kits, toy dishes, painting sets, and construction toys. For general fun, provide a wading pool, wooden trains, slides, and swings.

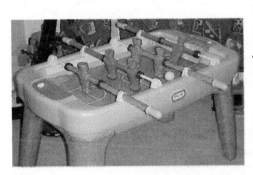

Young school-age children. Toys that please this age group include dolls and doll houses, games, craft and construction sets, blackboards, paints, hand puppets, mechanical action toys, jump ropes, balls, scooters, slides, swings, and tricycles.

You may have an opportunity to buy toys for a preschooler as a present, for the fun of it, or to help with the toy supply at the church nursery. Keep the following guidelines in mind when shopping for toys.

TOY SHOPPING GUIDELINES

The toy should be safe. Avoid sharp edges, toxic paint, and fragile, breakable toys.

The toy should be appropriate for the child's age and development.

The toy should challenge and interest the child, not frustrate him.

The toy should be worth the price. Toys that cost more should last longer.

The toy should be reliable. It should do what it is supposed to do.

The toy should be able to be used more than once.

The toy should be fun.

Children often like to play with household objects and enjoy a special treat on rainy days. Have some of the following items on hand to give the child a change from his ordinary play.

soap bubbles and pipe

gummed seals and paper

clay or play dough, cookie cutters, small rolling pin.

beads or colored macaroni to string

simple paper dolls

magnet

rubber stamp set and paper pipe cleaners

tape measure

blunt scissors, construction paper, old magazines, paste or tape

Match these items.

2.30 _____ push-pull toys   a. two-year-old

2.31 _____ rocking horse   b. three-year-old

2.32 _____ doll house   c. four-year-old

                                                   d. young school-age

Complete the following activities.

2.33   Select a toy and evaluate it. Rate the toy excellent, good, fair, or poor and explain your choice of rating.

Name of toy _____ Age level _____ Manufacturer _____

a. workability _____

_____

b. safety _____

_____

c. construction _____

_____

d. design _____

_____

FAMILY AND
CONSUMER SCIENCE

nine

LIFEPAC TEST

80/100

Name _____

Date _____

Score _____

FAMILY AND CONSUMER SCIENCE 09: LIFEPAC TEST

Matching (each blank, 2 points).

Physical (Answers may be used more than once.)

1. _____ most active stage in life
2. _____ developing large motor skills
3. _____ increases rapidly in height, weight, and motor skills
4. _____ good sense of balance and coordination

    a. infant
    b. toddler
    c. preschool
    d. young school-age

Intellect

5. _____ 300-word vocabulary
6. _____ can focus on and follow objects
7. _____ enjoys field trips
8. _____ one third of conversation is questions
9. _____ name body parts
10. _____ classification skills, reasoning ability development

    a. birth to 6 months
    b. one-year-old
    c. two-year-old
    d. three-year-old
    e. four-year-old
    f. young school-age

Social/Emotional

11. _____ feels empathy for others
12. _____ good time to experience separation
13. _____ cries to express anger, pain, hunger
14. _____ still needs security
15. _____ expresses anger by saying, "I hate you."

    a. birth to six months
    b. one-year-old
    c. two-year-old
    d. three-year-old
    e. four-year-old
    f. young school-age

Short Answer (answer, 5 points).

16. What are some of the spiritual truths a child can learn and understand?

_____

_____

_____

Answer *true* **or** *false* (each answer, 2 points).

17. _____ Each infant is a unique individual; different from other babies.

18. _____ Children are called toddlers when they are toilet trained.

19. _____ Two- and three-year-olds like to pretend.

20. _____ Infants will repeat actions that cause a response.

21. _____ Misbehavior may be an indication of boredom in a school-age child.

22. _____ Infants, six to twelve months old, cannot yet recognize right from wrong.

23. _____ The young school-age child prefers solitary play.

24. _____ Introduce books to children at an early age.

25. _____ Rice cereal is the first solid food that a baby eats.

26. _____ Scribbling is the first stage in artistic development.

27. _____ A child who likes the color blue, might color a picture of a dog blue.

28. _____ A heat exhaustion victim will have damp skin and high fever.

29. _____ A third degree burn is very painful.

30. _____ Proper hand washing prevents the spread of disease.

Fill in the blank (each answer, 3 points).

31. When picking up or holding a baby, you need to support the _____ and the _____ .

32. Finger foods help to develop _____ coordination.

33. The three areas of discipline are instruction, _____ , and _____ .

34. The three most highly contagious children's diseases are _____ , _____ , and _____ .

35. To stop a bleeding wound, you need to locate the source, apply _____ , _____ the wounded appendage and put pressure on the supplying artery.

Essay (answer, 7 points).

36. List the attributes that make a good babysitter in the eyes of the parent, from a business point of view, and in the eyes of the child.

    _____

    _____

    _____

    _____

    _____

NOTES

e. cost _____

_____

f. creativity _____

_____

Adult Check _____

Initial   Date

2.34 **Optional:** Make a stuffed toy for your brother, sister, cousin, or friend. Select a pattern from one of the major pattern companies. Follow the directions that come with the pattern. The toy should be washable. Sew all parts on securely; do not use glue. Use embroidery stitches for eyes, nose, and mouth if possible.

Adult Check _____

Initial   Date

Literature. Children can and should be introduced to books at an early age. All kinds of books are available for all age levels from cloth books and plastic picture books to children's novels.

Reading to children is an important part of their learning. Reading will help to develop their vocabulary, give them an appreciation for literature, and widen their horizons.

A good storybook will have the following qualities:

Introduce books to children from an early age.

—a theme
—a simple entertaining plot (an element of suspense or surprise is fun)
—something the child can identify with from his firsthand experience (for example, his puppy)
—well written sentences appropriate for the age level
—repetition, rhyming, play on words
—pictures that closely represent the written text
—teaches a principle, moral, or value which can be discussed with the child

Reading to a preschool child helps communicate your love for the child and demonstrates your interest in spending time with him. You and the child share the common world of the story. Reading to the child is a rewarding and relaxing experience. Also, reading to a child readies him for the task of learning to read.

Choose a story that the child likes. Read creatively and with expression. The child can tell if you are bored and uninterested. Sometimes it is fun to look through the book and talk about it, for example, "The train is going under the bridge and the cars are going on top of the bridge."

School-age children will want to read to you. Be patient and let them sound out the words they are unfamiliar with, helping only if you see they are becoming frustrated or ask for your help. It can be an exciting experience to see your child develop reading skills.

Answer the following question.

2.35 Why is it important to read to preschool children? _____

_____

_____

_____

Complete the following activity.

2.36 Write and illustrate a children's story.

Choose an age level _____

Decide on a theme _____

Using the guidelines for a good book, write your story in this LIFEPAC. Have your teacher check it. Make the necessary corrections.

Make a book from construction paper, dividing it into pages. Rewrite your story on the construction paper.

Illustrate each page. You may draw you own pictures or cut pictures out of magazines or photographs

Title: _____

Adult Check _____

Initial   **Date**

_____
title

_____

_____

_____

_____

_____

_____

_____

_____

_____

_____

Music. Music is a combination of tones or a rhythmic sequence of pleasing sounds. Children of all ages normally love music. For the child, music is relaxing, a method of releasing feelings, and a stimulus to movement. Music comforts the sad child and quiets the restless child. Music can teach the child about the world he lives in and the people he knows. Music can also be an outlet for a child's creativity. Music introduces the child to the love of God.

Children enjoy making music.

Music can be an integral part of the child's day. The child may like a special time to listen to a tape or CD, but music is not limited to any specific time. You and the child may sing while you are playing indoors or outdoors, while you are cleaning up, bathing, or while you are resting. Children love repetition and enjoy listening to and singing the same songs over and over.

Children also enjoy making their own music with rhythm instruments. Rhythm instruments help the child experiment with sound and gives the child freedom of body movement. School-age children may be ready to learn to play musical instruments.

 Complete the list.

2.37   List four benefits music has for the child.

a. _____

b. _____

c. _____

d. _____

Art. Art is a means of creative self-expression in a visual form. Children develop more relaxed attitudes and imaginative thinking if they are given opportunities for creative self-expression. The media, supervision, and experiences must be chosen wisely, keeping in mind how the child develops.

Medium. Art media used most often by young children include crayons, soap paint, tempera paint, finger paint, clay, Play-Doh®, collage pieces, and cutting and pasting. Provide the young child with plenty of space, time, and materials to work with.

Supervision. Supervision is necessary for the very young preschooler. Remember to protect the work surfaces and the child's clothing if the art experience is messy. Some art activities can be done outdoors when the weather is nice.

Experiences. Art experiences in early childhood will help the child do the following:

- use his imagination
- explore and discover different textures

- express his ideas for others to see
- learn to share materials
- make choices
- experience success and accomplishment

Scribbling is the first stage in artistic development. Scribbling begins around two years of age and lasts until four years of age. The younger preschool child receives satisfaction from the scribbling process, not from the finished picture. As the child develops his muscular control he will learn to place the lines where he wants them.

Around the age of four, the child's scribbling will begin looking like simple figures or objects. The child begins the symbolic stage of development. Children draw on the symbolic level until age eight. During the symbolic stage, the child may exaggerate parts of the picture that are most meaningful to him. For example, if the child just got a new toy, the toy in the picture may be oversized. Children like to use color, but they do not necessarily use it realistically. If the child likes red, he is likely to color his favorite things red, for example, his mother.

The following is a list of guidelines to help you work with and supervise art activities of young children. The guidelines can apply to all the art forms.

- Let the child work in his own way.
- Do not try to restrict him with any set pattern or design.
- Do not judge the artwork by adult standards.
- Display some of each child's artwork.
- Say, "Tell me about your picture," instead of "What is that?" It is obvious to the child what it is.
- Give sincere compliments to the child, "I like the way you used red in your picture."

Answer the question.

2.38   What is art? _____

_____

_____

Complete the following activities either individually or as a class.

2.39   Make finger paint and paint a picture.

> **These supplies will be needed:**
>
> 1 cup flour   spoon
> 1 tsp. salt   wintergreen extract (optional)
> 2 cups cold water   fingerpaint paper (banner or shelf
> 2 cups hot water   paper will do)
> food coloring   smock
> saucepan

Make the paint.

1. Mix the flour and salt with the two cups of cold water in the saucepan.

2. Add hot water and cook until mixture changes from white to a darker color.

3. Cool.

4. Add food coloring to the desired color. (A few drops of wintergreen extract will remove the flour smell.)

Paint the picture.

1. Wear a smock to protect your clothes.

2. Wet the fingerpaint paper.

3. Place a heaping spoonful of paint on the paper.

4. Pretend you are four years old and paint.

2.40   Make and use play dough.

> **These supplies will be needed:**
>
> | | |
> |---|---|
> | 2 cups flour | wax paper |
> | 1 cup salt | old cookie cutters |
> | food coloring | rolling pins |
> | water | toy hammer |
> | bowl | old garlic press |
> | zippered plastic bag | |

Make the dough.

1. Add enough water to flour and salt to mix it.

2. Add food coloring.

3. Keep the mixture from sticking. If this happens while the child is playing with the dough, add flour.

4. Store in a zippered plastic bag in the refrigerator.

Work with the play dough.

1. Place wax paper over the work surface.

2. Pretend you are three years old and roll, pound, tear, cut, bang, press, and play with your play dough.

Complete this activity.

2.41 **Observation number three.** Observe children participating in art activities. Watch and compare three children.

Date _____ Place _____ Age(s) of children _____

a. What age differences do you notice in the handling of materials?

_____

_____

_____

_____

b. How was interest in color demonstrated?

_____

_____

_____

c. Do the children talk to each other while working? What do they talk about?

_____

_____

_____

d. Does any one child ask for help more than the other children?

_____

_____

e. Were details included? How so?

_____

_____

_____

f. Discuss your observations with your teacher and classmates when back in class.

Adult Check _____

                                              Initial   **Date**

Science. Ecclesiastes 3:11 reads, "He [God] hath made every thing beautiful in His time...." As the young child watches and wonders about the world about him, he begins to ask questions about nature. He is experiencing science in his everyday life. Special science activities will help to teach the child about the orderliness of the universe and God's part in the universe, and will help to keep alive his sense of wonder at nature.

Concepts. Children are interested in all areas of science. Simple concepts introduced during the pre-school years are the foundation for more complex learning concepts during the school years. The following is a list of a few areas and simple concepts that are appropriate for young children.

Matter and energy

Air is around us.
We breathe air.
Machines work for us.

Living things and their activities

Living things need, air, water, warmth, and food.
Some plants grow from seeds; some from bulbs.
Some trees lose their leaves in the winter; others do not.
All animals have young animals.

Our earth and the universe

The moon, sun, and other stars are in the sky.
The sun gives light and heat.
God created the heaven and earth.
Man and his environment.
Man uses plants and animals for food and clothing.
Man uses animals for work and pleasure.
Man can travel in many ways.

Living things need, air, water, warmth, and food.

Activities. When you are babysitting or otherwise caring for children, you may want to prepare some science activities to supplement the children's play. Perhaps you can help the child grow a plant such as a sweet potato or plant some seeds outside for a small garden.

Children enjoy working in the garden.

Children enjoy field trips to see animals. As long as it is safe, children should be allowed to touch and feed animals. In the backyard, you may find a caterpillar, bird, cat, or dog. You may be able to go to a park and feed the ducks or visit the children's petting zoo.

Helping you cook is enjoyable for the young child. Stirring instant pudding, cutting out cookies, and buttering toast are all suitable for the young child. As you work together, discuss where the food comes from. Also, this is a good opportunity to discuss measurement and volume.

On a summer day, conducting sink/float experiments with a bucket of water is fun. Compare corks, balls, boats, rocks, nails, pieces of wood, pennies, and so forth.

Answer *true* **or** *false.*

2.42 _____ Science is part of the everyday life of a young child.

2.43 _____ Children should be allowed to touch and feed all animals.

2.44 _____ Cooking experiences help teach the child about his environment.

Complete the following activity.

2.45 You have been asked to design a science bulletin board for the three-year-olds' Sunday School class at your church. Choose one of the following verses as the theme and draw your bulletin board design in the space provided.

Psalms 74:17   Psalms 95:5
Psalms 102:25   Psalms 104:10
Psalms 104:14   Proverbs 20:12
Proverbs 27:26   John 1:3

Adult Check _____

SELF TEST 2

Answer *true* or *false*. If the answer is true, put *true* in the blank provided. If the answer is *false*, correct the underlined portion, and put the correct answer in the blank provided (each answer, 3 points).

2.01 _____ Introduce children to books <u>at an early age</u>.

2.02 _____ <u>Formula milk</u> provides all the nutrients a baby needs.

2.03 _____ <u>Cream of wheat</u> is the first solid food that a baby eats.

2.04 _____ The first step to bathing a baby is to <u>gather everything you are going to need</u>.

2.05 _____ By the time a child reaches school-age, <u>he no longer needs</u> to be held.

2.06 _____ Children have been known to drown in <u>only a couple of inches</u> of water.

2.07 _____ Submission needs to be learned in the <u>preschool stage</u> of life.

2.08 _____ Children should eat <u>2–4</u> servings of vegetables per day.

2.09 _____ <u>Scribbling</u> is the first stage in artistic development.

2.010 _____ Children <u>can</u> understand simple science concepts.

2.011 _____ Each child should <u>be expected to earn</u> your love.

Fill in the blank (each answer, 3 points).

2.012 When picking up or holding a baby, you need to support the _____ and the
_____ .

2.013 Finger foods help develop _____ coordination.

2.014 The best way to know if your child is eating properly is to follow the _____
guidelines.

Match the terms (each answer, 2 points).

2.015 _____ one third of conversation is questions   a. birth to six months

2.016 _____ discovers feet and hands   b. six months to one year

2.017 _____ understands more words than he can speak   c. two-year-old

2.018 _____ plays in small groups   d. three-year-old

e. four-year-old

f. young school-age

40

List (each answer, 4 points).

2.019 List four areas of science appropriate for children's study.

   a. _____

   b. _____

   c. _____

   d. _____

2.020 List four benefits of music for children.

   a. _____

   b. _____

   c. _____

   d. _____

2.021 List three art media appropriate for children.

   a. _____

   b. _____

   c. _____

Define (each answer, 3 points).

2.022 music

   _____

   _____

   _____

   _____

2.023 adventure play

   _____

   _____

   _____

   _____

III. SAFETY AND FIRST AID

And he sent them to preach the kingdom of God and to heal the sick.
Luke 9:2

Children are dependent on the people in charge of them to provide them with a healthy and safe environment. In this section of the LIFEPAC you will learn about safety precautions to help prevent accidents. You will study methods and techniques in handling minor health and injury problems. You will be able to recognize and treat three of the most common children's diseases.

Section Objective

Review this objective. When you have completed this section, you should be able to:

6.   Understand first aid and safety issues in child care.

PREVENTION

Accidents are the leading cause of death for people between the ages of 1 and 38. Keeping small children accident-free is a challenge. Every precaution should be taken to prevent accidents. When you are in charge of young children, follow as many of the following guidelines as possible.

+ Cover electrical outlets with plastic outlet protectors. Only use extension cords when absolutely necessary.

+ Keep all medicine out of the reach of children, and use a safety catch on the door. Children love to climb.

+ Keep medicine bottles tightly closed and use childproof lids.

+ Keep household cleaning products, insecticides, and other poisons in cabinets that little children cannot open.

+ Avoid using solid toilet bowl deodorizers that hang over the edge of the bowl.

+ Keep knives, scissors, and other sharp objects out of the sight and reach of children.

+ Be careful not to stack heavy items on unstable tables or stack things precariously on top of each other.

+ Look for sharp edges on furniture, cabinets, and wall decorations. Avoid protruding edges that could cause head, side, or other bodily injuries.

+ Have the outside play area free of rusty nails, loose broken boards, or other dangerous objects. There should be a locked, gated fence around the swimming pool.

+ Never leave a child alone in or near a swimming pool.

Never leave children unattended near swimming pools.

Have the following telephone numbers next to the phone in brightly colored, large print: doctor, poison control center, ambulance, hospital, pharmacy, police, fire, friend or relative to call for help, and a place where parents can be reached. In most areas, 911 covers fire, police, and paramedic emergency services.

Keep plastic bags out of the reach of children.

Keep old refrigerator, freezer or clothes dryer doors locked or remove them.

Have a supply of paper or unbreakable plastic cups and plates to use with children.

Keep matches out of the reach of children.

Teach children to wash hands properly. Dirty hands are responsible for the spread of many diseases.

Have first aid supplies handy.

Teach children to wash hands properly.

The first aid kit. Be sure to know the location of a first aid kit in your home, the homes where you babysit, at church, or anywhere else you care for children. A first aid kit should contain the following supplies:

a small roll of adhesive tape
gauze bandages
tweezers
safety pins
burn ointment
adhesive dressings in assorted
    sizes and shapes

absorbent cotton
small sharp scissors
clinical thermometer
wooden applicator sticks
antiseptic

Answer the following questions.

3.1   List three safety precautions for medication.

  a. _____

  b. _____

  c. _____

3.2   List two ways you can make the outside a safer environment.

  a. _____

  b. _____

3.3   List four telephone numbers that should be kept next to the phone.

  a. _____

  b. _____

  c. _____

  d. _____

3.4   What can be done to make old unused refrigerators, freezers, and clothes dryers safe? _____

  _____

3.5   What is one of the best ways to prevent the spread of diseases? _____

  _____

3.6   List six of the items that should be kept in a first aid kit.

  a. _____

  b. _____

  c. _____

  d. _____

  e. _____

  f. _____

PROBLEMS

Even though you do your best to provide for the safety of the children, accidents do happen. You will want to know how to handle minor accidents and how to deal with more serious ones. It is advisable to have a good first aid manual on hand. Also, taking first aid/CPR classes will enable you to handle virtually any emergency competently. Update the training periodically to keep yourself fresh and alert.

Allergic reactions. There are some people who are extremely sensitive to particular substances and who may suffer massive **systemic** reactions soon after exposure to them.

Some children are allergic to bee stings.

44

The acid from insect bites causes local inflammation and itching. Baking soda or soap will help reduce the itching. Administering acetaminophen (Tylenol®) eases the pain. Some children are allergic to the stings of bees, wasps, yellow jackets, and ants. Check with the parents for their instructions.

Signs of extreme **hypersensitivity (anaphylactic shock)** include:

a. sudden widespread blotchy, swelling of the skin; hives
b. difficulty in breathing; the airway may be shut off
c. wheezing
d. increased pulse rate
e. a sudden fall in blood pressure with a weak and thin pulse, nausea, vomiting, and abdominal cramps

> **What to do for a bee sting.**
> 1. Remove the stinger.
> 2. Apply ice, flush with cold water, or use a cold compress.
> 3. Apply calamine lotion to ease the itching and swelling.

These symptoms may quickly escalate into loss of consciousness and **cardiorespiratory** collapse. If untreated, they may lead rapidly to death. Anaphylactic shock is seen most commonly in response to insect stings, medications, or food.

Cuts, scrapes, and bruises. Children are constantly falling down and scraping a knee or elbow. Make sure you flush the wound with warm, soapy water and apply an antiseptic cream or ointment before affixing a bandage. Bruises should have ice applied to them to help reduce swelling.

Bleeding. More serious bleeding wounds should be taken care of as follows:

a. Locate the source of the bleeding. Remember, head wounds bleed a great deal no matter how extensive the damage. Don't panic.
b. Use a *clean* folded cloth and apply direct pressure to the wound.
c. Elevate the wounded appendage.
d. Check to see if the bleeding has stopped. If the bleeding has stopped, wrap the wound with gauze. If not, call or take him to the doctor.
e. If the bleeding is severe, apply pressure on the supplying artery.

Nose bleeds are another common problem with children. To stop nose bleeds, have the child sit down, do not have him lay down. His head should be either upright or tilted forward slightly. Pinch the nose on the side that is bleeding, or if both sides are bleeding, pinch toward the bridge of the nose. A cold compress may be helpful. If the bleeding still doesn't stop, put a tissue up the nostril. If severe bleeding persists after 15 minutes and you are unable to stop it, take the child to the hospital so the medical staff can pack the nose.

Burns. Burns can be caused by fire, heated liquid, steam, chemicals, the sun, and electricity. The severity of a burn is determined by which of the three layers of skin has been affected. A first-degree burn is the least severe; the epidermis or outer layer of the skin is red, tender, and painful, but there is no swelling or blisters. A second-degree burn involves both the epidermis and dermis; the middle layer of the skin is red, tender, painful, and blistered. A third-degree burn, always serious, involves destruction of all thicknesses of the skin. The color is black or white, but there is no pain because the nerves have been destroyed. Seek medical help immediately.

Hold minor burns under cool water until the stinging stops. Never use butter, oil, or ointments on a burn. For more serious burns, apply a dry sterile dressing and call the doctor. Have the victim drink plenty of fluids, because a burn robs the body of fluids by drawing those fluids to the burn. Don't break the blisters; they are used in the healing process. Breaking the blisters also opens up the burned area to infection.

Teach a child to stop, drop, and roll so he will know what to do if he ever catches on fire. Have the child stop running and cover his face, drop to the ground, and immediately roll over and over, putting out any flames.

Chemical burns need to be flushed with cold water for fifteen minutes. If the chemical should enter an eye, remember to turn the head with burned eye down, so the water does not run into the good eye and contaminate it as well. Cover the eye with a clean cloth and go to the doctor immediately. Be sure to know the name of the chemical to tell the doctor.

Seizures. A child may have a sudden attack due to epilepsy or some other disorder. Make a soft area on the floor and roll the child to the side so his saliva can drain from his mouth. Don't restrain him or put anything in his mouth, such as a pencil. Keep the child from swallowing his tongue. If the seizure continues for more than a few minutes, or if it recurs within a short period of time, call for an ambulance.

Fainting. Fainting is caused when blood supply to the brain is inadequate. Help the person to lie on his back. Check breathing, then check the **carotid** artery for a pulse.

Raising the legs is important, because it increases the blood supply to the heart and head, therefore increasing the blood supply to the brain. Do not give the person an alcoholic drink or splash cold water on his or her face. A cold compress may be applied to the forehead.

Fever. A fever is an elevation of a person's body temperature by one or two degrees. You should know how to use a thermometer. Digital thermometers are now widely available, as are ones that can be placed in an ear. These have easy to read displays. If the temperature is elevated, check for other signs of illness: upset stomach, earache, chills, nausea and such to help determine the best path to take to help the child.

Foreign bodies. Children are always placing small objects into parts of the body where they do not belong. The following are a few pointers for removing foreign objects from the eye, ear, and nose.

Eyes

    a. Wash your hands carefully.
    b. Gently pull the lower lid down.
    c. With a slightly moistened cotton swab or the corner of a clean handkerchief, lift off the foreign body.
    d. Flush the eye with lukewarm water.

Ears

    a. Never attempt to remove a foreign object that has entered the ear canal by poking it with a matchstick, pencil, cotton swab, or similar device.
    b. A soft object not deeply embedded and clearly visible may be withdrawn carefully with tweezers.
    c. If unable to remove the object safely, then take the person to the doctor.

Nose

    a. Do not inhale forcefully through the nose. Rather, have the person breathe through the mouth.
    b. Gently blow the nose a couple of times to dislodge the object.
    c. If the object is visible, use tweezers to remove it.
    d. If unable to remove the object safely, take the person to the doctor.

Sprains. A sprained joint has had its ligaments and fibers over-stretched and partly torn by a sudden forceful movement. A cold **compress** is helpful if applied immediately. Keep the joint elevated and at rest. After twenty minutes replace, the compress with a thick bandage to provide firm support. An elastic bandage is helpful.

Fractures. There is really very little you can do to repair injuries to bones, muscles, and connective tissues. The best you can do is to judge the nature of the injury, get medical aid for the injured person, and keep the situation from worsening. Immobilization avoids further injury and aids in the prevention of further pain.

Sun and heat. Overexposure to heat and humidity may lead to heat cramps, heat exhaustion, or heat stroke. Heat cramps occur as a result of salt and water loss through perspiring. Replenishing supplies of salt and water should alleviate the cramps. Drinking electrolyte solutions (Gatorade®) is also helpful. Stretching the cramped muscle may give immediate relief.

A victim of heat exhaustion will be pale; his body temperature will be normal or only modestly elevated, and the skin will be damp. He may suffer from nausea, weakness, and light-headedness. Move the victim to a cool, shady or air conditioned place; loosen or remove most of the clothing, and give him plenty of fluids.

The most serious result of overexposure to heat and humidity is heat stroke. Heat stroke is considered a medical emergency, so call 911 immediately. There may be damage to internal organs. The victim will feel hot to touch and the skin will be red and dry. His temperature will be 106° Fahrenheit and he will not be sweating. Other symptoms may include rapid heartbeat, confusion, agitation, lethargy, stupor, and loss of consciousness. The victim should be moved to a cooler place. Cool the victim down by covering him with cold, wet sheets, and continue monitoring his temperature. A fan will increase the heat loss.

Poisons. Children are inclined to consume all sorts of substances adults would never consider putting in their mouths. Call your local poison center immediately. Give the victim a large glass of water or milk to dilute the poison if so instructed by poison center personnel. Be prepared to give the poison center the following information: age of victim, type of poison, and amount consumed, first aid being given, information as to whether the person has vomited. If the victim is unconscious, keep the airway open. Save the poison container and any sample of vomitus available to take along when going for medical assistance.

Do not induce vomiting if the following poisons have been swallowed: ammonia, lye products, sulfuric, nitric or hydrochloric acids, benzene, liquid furniture and metal polish, turpentine, or oven cleaner. These will cause the esophagus to burn should the child vomit.

The safest **emetic** is syrup of ipecac.

Aspirin is the most common cause of accidental poisoning of children. A bottle of 50 children's aspirin tablets can kill a child.

Puncture wounds. Puncture wounds are wounds caused by sharp, slender objects such as a needle, nail, or splinter. The majority can be handled by cleansing with soap and water. A tetanus immunization should be given if needed (your doctor should have record of your last tetanus shot). At the first sign of redness, swelling, increased pain or fever, consult your doctor.

Sore throat. A sore throat may be the result of a viral infection and will respond to treatment or it may be a symptom of a far more serious disorder. Strep throat (presence of streptococcus bacteria) is usually accompanied by high fever and difficulty in swallowing. It could lead to rheumatic fever or kidney inflammation. Treatment for viral sore throat consists of rest, non-aspirin pain and fever reliever, warm saline water gargles, and plenty of fluids.

A
B **Answer the following questions.**

3.7　How do you treat an insect bite? _____

_____

3.8　The three most common things that can cause anaphylactic shock are:

　　a.　_____

　　b.　_____

　　c.　_____

3.9　Before applying a bandage on a cut or scrape, one should first _____

_____ .

3.10　To reduce swelling of bruises apply _____ .

3.11　Stop a wound from bleeding by _____

_____

_____ .

3.12　Where do you pinch the nose if both nostrils are bleeding? _____

3.13　Describe how you would care for a minor burn._____

_____

_____

3.14　Distinguish between first-, second-, and third-degree burns._____

_____

_____

_____

3.15　Distinguish between heat exhaustion and heat stroke. _____

_____

_____

3.16　What is syrup of ipecac? _____

3.17　How do you treat a chemical burn? _____

_____

_____

3.18　Name two things that can be done if a child feels faint. _____

_____

3.19 What is the best way to remove a foreign body from the nose? _____

_____

3.20 Apply a _____ to a sprain before bandaging.

3.21 Strep throat is an example of a _____ infection.

THREE COMMON CHILDREN'S DISEASES

Head lice. Head lice are most often found in children from ages 3–10. Some people estimate head lice is the second most common infection experienced by children next to the common cold.

Head lice make their home in human hair. In only two weeks, a louse can lay as many as 120 eggs, known as nits. They attach to the shaft of hair, close to scalp and hairline, usually at the back of the head or above and behind the ears. When head lice are alive and living, they inject a small amount of saliva under the skin; the injection of this saliva causes itching.

The first sign of head lice is an extremely itchy head. If your child has lice, you will see little white or tan nits in his hair. Nits are discreet dots that are usually stuck onto the shaft of the hair and are very difficult to remove.

Getting rid of lice is time-consuming. First, shampoo the hair with lice shampoo. Then, comb the hair with the special comb provided with the shampoo. This is tedious, but you must remove all nits. Then disinfect by washing all clothing and bedding or anything that the infected child has been near.

Pink eye. Pink eye is the most common eye disorder in the Western Hemisphere. It is defined as a contagious, epidemic form of acute conjunctivitis occurring in humans; so called from the color of the inflamed eye. Conjunctivitis is the inflammation of the delicate membrane lining the eyelids and covering the eyeball. Sign of pink eye are red **sclera**, sticky discharge, itching, and pain. Pink eye usually begins in one eye and quickly spreads to the other by contamination of touch, washcloths, or one's own hand.

Treatment is simple. Wash your hands properly and often. Do not rub or put objects into your eye. Apply warm compresses and therapeutic ointment or drops. A physician may prescribe a special ointment.

Chickenpox. Chickenpox (varicella) can occur at any age, but most commonly are ages 2-8. It is transmitted by direct contact (primarily respiratory secretions or skin **lesions**) and indirect contact. The **incubation** period for chickenpox is 13-17 days. It is **communicable** one day before lesions erupt to six days after **vesicles** form. It is most contagious in the early stages of eruption of skin lesions. It affects all races and both sexes equally. Most children recover completely.

Before any rash appears, the child may have a slight fever, display of weakness or discomfort, and no appetite. Within 24 hours, the rash begins as crops of small red berry-like spots and progresses to clear vesicles with red around the edge. Then, finally the scabs form.

The best treatment for chickenpox is strict isolation until all the vesicles and most of the scabs have disappeared, usually one week from the onset of the rash. Some relief can be found by using calamine lotion, taking Benadryl, and taking a cool bath with baking soda or epsom salt in the water.

It is better to have the chickenpox while still a child. It can be much more severe for an adult. Normally once you have had chickenpox, you will not get it again. In 1995 the Food and Drug Administration approved a vaccine for chickenpox. Doctors recommend children receive this vaccine around 12 months and a booster around age 13.

Answer the following questions.

3.22   Head lice is most often found in children from ages _____ .

3.23   Why does the head itch so much when head lice are present? _____

_____

3.24   What is pink eye? _____

_____

3.25   How would you treat pink eye? _____

_____

3.26   Chickenpox can occur at any age, but most common are ages _____ .

3.27   Define communicable. _____

_____

3.28   The incubation period for chickenpox is _____ days.

Answer *true* **or** *false*.

3.29   _____   It is better to have chickenpox as a child than as an adult.

Review the material in this section in preparation for the Self Test. This Self Test will check your mastery of this particular section as well as your knowledge of the previous sections.

SELF TEST 3

Answer *true* **or** *false* (each answer, 3 points).

3.01 _____ The two-year-old is old enough to share his toys.

3.02 _____ Four-year-olds have a vocabulary of about 300 words.

3.03 _____ Baking soda is good to use on an ant bite.

3.04 _____ Proper hand washing prevents the spread of disease.

3.05 _____ Suntan lotion should be a part of your first aid kit.

3.06 _____ When holding a baby, you should support the head and the back.

3.07 _____ Bottle feeding helps develops hand to mouth coordination.

3.08 _____ Introduce books to children at an early age.

3.09 _____ Keep the phone number of the Poison Control Center near the telephone.

3.010 _____ Begin to teach submission to the toddler.

Fill in the blank (each answer, 2 points).

3.011 Accidents are the leading cause of death for people between the ages of _____ and _____ .

3.012 Anaphylactic shock is seen most commonly in response to _____ , medications, or food.

3.013 To stop a bleeding wound, you need to locate the source, apply _____ , _____ the wounded appendage, and put pressure on the supplying artery.

3.014 Teach a child to _____ , _____ , and _____ so that they will know what to do if they catch on fire.

3.015 The safest emetic is _____ .

Short Answer (each answer, 5 points).

3.016 List and describe the three kinds of burns.

    a. _____

    _____

    b. _____

    _____

    c. _____

    _____

3.017   How can you tell if a victim is suffering from heat exhaustion or heat stroke?

_____

_____

_____

_____

3.018. List the three most common highly contagious children's diseases.

a. _____

b. _____

c. _____

3.019   What do you do for a cut or scrape? _____

_____

_____

3.020   How do you treat a chemical burn to the eye? _____

_____

_____

3.021   What do you do if a child feels faint? _____

_____

_____

78
98

Score _____

Adult Check _____

Initial   Date

IV. THE BUSINESS OF BABYSITTING

No matter what task you take on, it is important to remember *Who* you are representing. In order to glorify God in your babysitting business, you must be fair, diligent, honest, and loving.

Babysitting is both a privilege and an incredible responsibility. You have a job to do and someone is paying you for your time. Knowing what makes a good babysitter, what the business aspects to babysitting are, and what the parent's expectations are will help you become a babysitter that is in demand. This section of the LIFEPAC will help you identify these aspects of babysitting.

Section Objective

Review this objective. When you have completed this section, you should be able to:

7.   Become a responsible and successful babysitter.

CHARACTERISTICS OF A DEPENDABLE BABYSITTER

Parents look for certain qualities in a reliable babysitter. They expect the babysitter to be in good health. If you have a cold or other contagious disease, do not accept a babysitting job or call and cancel a previously arranged babysitting job. Recommend another reliable person to substitute for you so the parents won't be in a bind at the last minute.

The parents expect the babysitter to be dependable and responsible. Dependability is a must; involves following through with your commitment and being on time. Other than sickness or a family emergency, there is no excuse for cancellation. Responsibility involves diligent and loving care for their child's health and safety. It is your responsibility to get the necessary instructions for the child's care.

A good sitter enjoys children.

Parents look for a babysitter who loves little children. The best babysitters usually understand and are comfortable around children. Children tend to know whether you like them or not.

A dependable babysitter should be self confident. Children judge you as much by the way you look and act as by the words you say. Be sure of yourself.

You need to be mature. Be levelheaded and act calmly in case of an emergency. You have to maintain authority and discipline.

A good babysitter will show good manners. Be pleasant and act in a courteous manner. This includes respect for the privacy of families by not going through closets and their personal possessions.

Be knowledgeable about children. You need a basic understanding of the stages of child development. You must also know the basic techniques of feeding, dressing, diapering, bathing, and playing with both younger and older children.

Maintain a professional attitude. Make sure you agree on the business aspects of the job before babysitting with a new family for the first time. Get the necessary information from the parents before they leave.

Be adaptable. Accept the fact that families are different. The way things are done in the house where you are baby-sitting may be different from your own house. Accept those differences between households. It is your responsibility to fit in with the family's usual pattern or routines—not the other way around. If you feel uncomfortable with the family's lifestyle, you may need to refuse to accept the opportunity to work for them.

Be safety conscious. Protect the children from harm. Be alert at all times. Good babysitters take extra precautions to make sure the children are safe from accidents. If you need to talk on the phone, make sure you always know where the children are. Keep calls brief and always be attentive to the children. For safety guidelines, see the chart on the following page.

Good babysitters are always in demand.

You will be in demand. Word gets around; conscientious babysitters are known by many parents. Usually these sitters are busy with repeat jobs for the same families.

Answer the following questions.

4.1   What are two qualities that parents look for in a good babysitter?

     a. _____

     b. _____

4.2   Maturity is important so that you as the babysitter can maintain _____ and

     _____ .

4.3   A good babysitter will respect the _____ of the families by not going through

     _____ and _____ possessions.

4.4   The babysitter needs a basic understanding of the _____ of child development.

4.5   In what respect should you be adaptable in your babysitting jobs? _____

     _____

CHILD SAFETY GUIDELINES

✗ Never leave a young child alone while he/she is awake. Check on the child occasionally while he is sleeping.

✗ Never leave a baby unattended on a changing table, in a high chair, bath, or walker. Use safety straps whenever they are available.

✗ Stay awake so you will hear the children if they need you.

✗ Children will likely try you out to see how far you will let them go. Be firm in insisting that they play where they will be safe.

✗ Closets, medicine chests, drawers, and storage locations are not proper places for children to play. Also keep them away from stairways, hot objects (such as an iron or curling iron), stoves, microwaves, and electrical outlets.

✗ Keep scissors, knives, or other sharp objects out of sight.

✗ Keep buttons, pins, money, small toy pieces, matches, and any other small particles off the floor and out of sight.

✗ If playing outdoors, know where their parents permit them to play. Watch for traffic and fire hazards, garden sprays, tools, and unfriendly animals.

✗ Don't bathe the children unless specifically asked to do so. If you do bathe the children, do it very carefully and never leave a child unattended. The water in the bathtub should be comfortable to touch, not too hot!

✗ Cut food into bite sized pieces for toddlers and preschoolers.

✗ Make sure that children remain seated while eating.

✗ Try to avoid foods that are likely to cause a young child to choke such as popcorn, hot dogs, hard candy, or grapes.

✗ Make sure that doors to rooms such as the bathroom, basement, and garage are closed.

✗ Remove plastic bags, beanbags, or pillows that could cover a child's face and cut off breathing.

✗ Remove any strings or straps from items that may pose a strangulation hazard to a young child.

ESSENTIAL BUSINESS PRACTICES

You have a job to do and someone is paying you for your time. This is not a time to invite a friend in or have a lengthy phone call. If you do need to call someone, limit your conversation to a few minutes. It is important to keep the line open for parents to call home or for someone else who has an important message. You should never have visitors unless special arrangements have been made with the parents.

Leave the house in good order; it should be as clean, if not cleaner, than it was when you arrived. If dishes have been used, wash and rinse them. Help the children pick up toys and games with which they have played.

Messages for the parents should be taken accurately. Parents should also receive a brief report about the children's behavior and any unusual happenings. Most parents want an accurate account, so don't try to protect the children from parental discipline.

To prevent a misunderstanding, both the sitter and the parents need to make some business arrangements prior to baby-sitting for the first time. Some of the questions to discuss include:

Financial Arrangements. What is a fair rate of pay? Check with others who baby-sit in your community. Talk with your parents. Ask yourself these questions: Do you charge by the hour or the job? Do you charge the same for every family and every job?

How do you state your charges and collect your money? The time to discuss the fee is when you accept the sitting date. After discussing the job, just say "I charge _____ an hour." Your working time begins when you arrive and ends when the parents return home. Make a note of the time, figure the total hours, and be prepared to give the amount. Most parents will ask "How much do we owe you?" Be prepared to say: "That is three hours at _____ an hour, so it is _____ ."

General Expectations. The following are questions you should consider before establishing your baby-sitting business. What is the expected time period that you will be baby-sitting? How many hours? Will it be a regular schedule—daily, weekly or another time arrangement? How late can you stay? Will you baby-sit during the week or weekends only?

If you are babysitting on a daily basis, you should consider other more involved questions such as these: Will you be required to do any special tasks such as washing dishes or light cleaning? Will you be expected to transport children to and from school, sporting events, school or church events?

How will you get to their home and back again? You should not have to walk home alone at night even for a short distance. You may not be comfortable riding alone with a particular adult and/or riding in a car that is being driven by an intoxicated parent. The best solution may be to have your own parents drop you off and pick you up again. Tell your parents *immediately* if a parent acts inappropriately with you and do not babysit there again.

If you find that you are expected to do an unreasonable amount of work that was not mentioned in your arrangements, you may need to cross this family off your list.

 Answer the questions.

4.6   What are three reasons that it is not a good idea to spend time on the phone while babysitting?

  a. _____

  b. _____

  c. _____

4.7   What are four things you should consider from a business perspective?

  a. _____

  b. _____

  c. _____

  d. _____

INFORMATION YOU NEED

When you take a babysitting job, there is important information you need to get from the parents. You will need a list of emergency numbers such as fire, police, ambulance (911 generally takes care of all three), doctors, neighbors, and family members. Be sure you know the address and phone number of the house, including the major cross streets, when you're watching children to relay to the 911 operator, should an emergency arise.

It is wise to know how to reach the parent in case of an emergency. Get the name, address and telephone number of where the parents are going. Ask for the cell phone number and/or pager number if available. Find out the time they expect to get to their destination and when they expect to arrive. If they are going to more than one place, get the approximate time they will switch locations. If they are going to see a play or listen to a concert, get the row and seat numbers of their tickets. Find out what time they expect to return home.

It is a good policy to obtain information as to whether they are expecting any phone calls or visitors. If they are, then you need to find out who and when they should call or arrive. Inquire as to how the parents would like the door and phone to be answered (if at all).

You should get information concerning any specifics in the care of the child(ren).

The information about the child(ren) should include:

Meals and Menus—When is mealtime? What should the child(ren) eat? Are there any food allergies or restrictions? May he have a snack? What can he eat for a snack? Ask what you may eat and only eat what you are told. Does the child have any eating problems or dislikes? How much should he eat?

Medication—Do not give the child any medication unless instructed by the parents. Have them write down the name of the medication, the correct dosage, the time it should be given, and if food or a drink should be avoided or given with the medication.

HOUSEHOLD SAFETY

—Keep windows and outside doors locked, and do not open them to see who is there.

—Be careful not to offer information over the phone. **Do not** tell anyone that you are alone.

—Keep the radio or TV turned low so that you can hear a cry or call from the child when he/she is sleeping.

—Put things away and out of reach of children when preparing food.

—Always know where the emergency exits are located.

—Look for potential hazards in the home such as open stairways, uncovered electrical outlets, or sharp objects that are within reach.

—Keep gates across stairways to prevent falls from occurring.

—Keep children from playing near glass doors and windows.

—Put medicine, cleaning products, pesticides, paint, and plants up so they are out of reach of young children. Many of these items can be quite dangerous.

—If there is an emergency, call 911.

Playtime—Are there special play areas inside the house? Are the children allowed to play outside? Are playmates allowed in the yard or house? Is the child allowed to go to a friend's house? Which friends and what is the address and phone number? Does the child have any special jobs to do—any special requirements? Are any toys to be avoided? Can he play on the computer? If yes, what programs can he use and are there instructions for starting them? Can he watch TV? If yes, how long can he watch and what programs can he watch?

Bedtime—When is bedtime? Have there been any problems getting the child to go to bed? Is there a favorite story or bedtime friend? Security blanket or pacifier? Where is he to sleep? Does he have a special bedtime routine? If yes, what is it? What clothes should he wear to bed?

Bath time—Do you need to give the child a bath? If yes, does he take a bath or shower? Can he clean his body and shampoo his hair without help? Can he brush his teeth without help? What clothes should he wear after bathing? Remember to never leave a child alone in a bathtub with water!

Discipline—Are there any house rules that you need to know before the parents depart? Do parents expect you to discipline their child when he is misbehaving? If so, what type of behaviors would require disciplinary action and what method would they want you to use? Are parents wanting you to report any misbehavior from the child upon their arrival home?

If you are going to provide for the safety and proper care of the children then there is vital information you need to obtain about the house. It should include:

Locks, Alarms, and Extra Keys—Where are they? How do they work? How do the windows work?

Emergency Supplies—Ask about flashlights, candles and matches, first aid, and cleaning supplies.

Appliances—Make sure you know how to work the can opener, stovetop and oven, microwave, high chair, infant swing, and anything else you may need while you're watching the children. Ask how to adjust the heat or air conditioning.

Pets—If the family has pets, check to see if they need to be fed or given water. When, what, and how much? Can they go outside? Are they allowed on the furniture or in bed with the child?

Miscellaneous—Take a tour of the home. Find out where everything you'll need is located. Determine the quickest route of escape from children's rooms in case of fire or other emergency.

PERSONAL SAFETY

Don't let haste or carelessness cause you to have an accident.

Carry the baby or any package so that you can see where you are walking.

If you should suffer a cut or burn put the baby in his crib and take other children with you while you administer first aid.

If you are annoyed, bothered, or in doubt about any unusual people or situations, call one of the people you are to contact in emergencies or your own parents.

If you get sick while babysitting, call your parents or another qualified babysitter to take over for you. Then contact the parents to let them know of the change in plans for their final approval.

Answer the following.

4.8   *True* or *False* It is inappropriate to ask where the parents are going and when they will be home.

_____

4.9   List the six areas you should get information from the parent concerning the care of the child.

_____

_____

_____

4.10   What are three things you can do to provide a safer environment and prepare for an emergency?

_____

_____

_____

BABYSITTER'S CHECKLIST

The chart below can be duplicated for your future use. It is advisable to have all the information filled in for the safety of the children you care for and for your own safety as well.

Babysitting can be a great way to earn some money, but remember, you have the lives of others in your safekeeping. That is an enormous responsibility. The welfare of the child must come first.

THE BABYSITTER'S CHECKLIST

1. Address of the house _____
2. Phone number at the house _____
3. Name and phone of family doctor _____
4. Emergency services phone number(s) (if not 911) _____
5. Hospital name and phone number _____
6. Poison Control phone number _____
7. Where the parents will be (address) _____
8. Phone number where the parents can be reached _____
9. Cell phone or pager number(s) for parents _____
10. What time the parents are expected home _____
11. Name of neighbors _____
12. Phone number of neighbors _____
13. Name of grandparents or other close relative _____
14. Phone number of grandparents /relative _____
15. Any items that need special attention _____
16. Any allergies or special medical information for children _____

_____

_____

Before you take this last Self Test, you may want to do one or more of these self checks.

1. _____ Read the objectives. Determine if you can do them.

2. _____ Restudy the material related to any objectives that you cannot do.

3. _____ Use the SQ3R study procedure to review the material:
   a. **S**can the sections.
   b. **Q**uestion yourself again.
   c. **R**ead to answer your questions.
   d. **R**ecite the answers to yourself.
   e. **R**eview areas you didn't understand.

4. _____ Review all vocabulary, activities, and Self Tests, writing a correct answer for each wrong answer.

SELF TEST 4

Choose the best answer (each answer, 3 points).

4.01. An individual generally grows most rapidly physically during _____ .
   a. the first year of life
   b. the preschool years
   c. the elementary school years
   d. adolescence

4.02 Most young children prefer foods which are _____ .
   a. strongly flavored
   b. served very hot
   c. highly seasoned
   d. easily eaten with fingers

4.03 Just before a young child goes to bed, it is best to _____ .
   a. play an active game
   b. threaten him
   c. read a pleasant story to him
   d. watch an exciting TV show

4.04 Effective discipline involves _____ .
   a. physical punishment
   b. telling a child what he cannot do
   c. establishing acceptable behavior
   d. bribing the child

Short Answer (each answer, 6 points).

4.05 At what age are most children toilet trained; at least during the daytime? _____

4.06 What is the most important thing to remember when holding a newborn baby? _____

_____

_____

4.07 How does one effectively create a love for books in young children? _____

_____

_____

List (each answer, 5 points).

4.08 As a babysitter, what are three things you should consider from a business perspective?

   a. _____

   b. _____

   c. _____

4.09 What are three characteristics of a dependable babysitter?

a. _____

b. _____

c. _____

4.010 List three safety rules for babysitting.

a. _____

b. _____

c. _____

4.011 List two areas you should get information from the parent concerning the care of the child.

a. _____

b. _____

4.012 List three of your responsibilities to the child as a babysitter.

a. _____

b. _____

c. _____

<table>
<tr><td>80 / 100</td></tr>
</table>

Score _____

Adult Check _____
                Initial   Date

Before taking the LIFEPAC Test, you may want to do one or more of these self checks.

1. _____ Read the objectives. Check to see if you can do them.
2. _____ Restudy the material related to any objectives that you cannot do.
3. _____ Use the SQ3R study procedure to review the material.
4. _____ Review activities, Self Tests, and LIFEPAC vocabulary words.
5. _____ Restudy areas of weakness indicated by the last Self Test.

GLOSSARY

adventure play. The overcoming of obstacles—climbing, jumping, crawling, balancing.

anaphylactic shock. A hypersensitive reaction that can occur after a person has had exposure to a toxin such as several bee stings.

barrier cream. A cream applied to protect the skin from moisture. A commonly known over-the-counter brand is Desitin™.

cardiorespiratory collapse. Failure of both heart and lungs to function properly, or to shut down completely.

carotid. Either of the two arteries that carry oxygenated blood from the aorta to the head. It is the vessel you check in the neck for a pulse.

communicable. Capable of being easily transmitted.

compress. A soft cloth pad held in place by a bandage and used to provide pressure or to supply moisture, cold, heat or medication.

cooperative play. The child cooperates and plays with one or more children, sharing and taking turns.

creative play. Playing with materials on which a child can use his imagination—wood blocks, paint, clay.

emetic. A substance used to induce vomiting.

hypersensitivity. Allergic to a substance to which a normal individual does not react.

imaginative play. Dramatic play—dressing up in clothes, pretending.

incubation. The time it takes the eggs to hatch.

lesions. An injury, hurt, wound.

manipulative skills. Skills using hands, such as those using jigsaw puzzles, color and shape —matching sets, scissors, hammers, screwdrivers.

parallel play. Where a child plays alongside another child but not with him; children may be doing the same activity, for example, blocks.

phytochemicals. Plant chemicals or nutrients.

representational. One that represents a likeness or image.

reprimand. Severe admonishment or scolding.

sclera. A dense, white fibrous membrane that, with the cornea, forms the external covering of the eyeball.

secondhand learning. Reading or telling stories, looking at books, pictures, listening to records, educational television.

solitary play. The child plays alone; he is interested in his own activities, his own toys.

systemic. Pertaining to or affecting the entire bodily system or the entire body as a whole.

vesicles. Blisters.

viral. Pertaining to or caused by a virus.

wean (weaning). To accustom a child or animal to food other than its mother's milk.

BIBLIOGRAPHY

Barclay, Marion, S., *Teen Guide to Homemaking*, Third edition, McGraw Hill, NY, 1972.

City of Manhattan Beach, CA, police department, *Babysitting Safety Tips/Checklist*, http://www.ci.manhattan-beach, ca.us/police/crime-prevention/babysit.html., 2000.

Hoehn, Robert G., *Practical First Aid Skill Builders*.

Leiter, Gila, MD and Babbitz, Allen H., MD, *Labor of Love*, Mosby-Yearbook Inc., NY, 1998.

Urban Program Resource Network, http://www.urbanext.uiuc.edu/, The University of Illinois Extension, *A guide to the business of babysitting, 2000.*

Webmaster@GuardianAlarm.com, *The BabySitter's Checklist*, last updated, Sept. 1999.